PATHWAYS TO RECOVERY AND DESISTANCE

The Role of the Social Contagion of Hope

David Best

First published in Great Britain in 2019 by

Policy Press
University of Bristol
1-9 Old Park Hill
Bristol
BS2 8BB
UK
t: +44 (0)117 954 5940
pp-info@bristol.ac.uk
www.policypress.co.uk

North America office:
Policy Press
c/o The University of Chicago Press
1427 East 60th Street
Chicago, IL 60637, USA
t: +1 773 702 7700
f: +1 773 702 9756
sales@press.uchicago.edu
www.press.uchicago.edu

British Library Cataloguing in Publication Data
A catalogue record for this book is available from the British Library.

Library of Congress Cataloging-in-Publication Data
A catalog record for this book has been requested.

ISBN 978-1-4473-4930-3 paperback
ISBN 978-1-4473-4932-7 ePub
ISBN 978-1-4473-4931-0 OA PDF

Cover design by Clifford Hayes
Printed and bound by CPI Group (UK) Ltd, Croydon, CR0 4YY
Policy Press uses environmentally responsible print partners

MIX
Paper | Supporting responsible forestry
FSC® C013604
FSC
www.fsc.org

Contents

List of figures and table

Figures

Table

Acknowledgements and dedication

There are many people to thank for this book and I hope that I have done them all justice with what I have produced.

As I reviewed the draft for this book, I realised just how many of the people I mention in here have been friends and inspirations in my work – from Australia, Gerard Byrne and Pauline Spencer; and from the UK, Steve Hodgkins and Graham Beck in Blackpool and Kirkham; Stuart Green from Doncaster and my other colleagues from Recovery Cities, Charlotte Colman, Linda Nilsson and Mulka Nisic; Stephen Youdell from Double Impact.

I would also like to acknowledge and thank the support I have received from a wonderful group of PhD students, Lauren Hall, Beth Collinson, Kieran Lynch, Zeddy Chaudhry and Rebecca Hamer, as well as any number of colleagues in Australia and the UK.

Academically, I would like to take this opportunity to thank three of the people who have guided and inspired me throughout my academic career – Professor Dwayne Simpson of Texas Christian University, William White of Chestnut Health Systems and Professor John Braithwaite from Australian National University. They have inspired and supported me at key times throughout my career.

There are also numerous other people who have been kind enough to dedicate their time and attention to my work through their own personal belief in recovery, rehabilitation and the idea that people can become 'better than well'.

Finally, I would like to thank my family who have shown patience and incredible depths of support and understanding.

Ultimately, however, I want to dedicate this book to my son, Billy. I love you.

Foreword

Traditional folklore suggests that the trajectory of drug addiction shifts from self-accelerating drug use to recovery initiation when the pain of continued use becomes greater than the anticipated pain of drug cessation. Desistance from criminal offending has been similarly viewed as a function of untoward consequences and the fear of greater consequence. Both theories of change posit the power of pain and punishment as THE primary push factor in behavioural change, and both have exerted a profound influence on international policies related to drug use and criminal conduct. Professor David Best is one of the leading pioneers suggesting a quite alternative view – one extolling the power of pull factors (for example, community connection, hope, identity reconstruction, life meaning and purpose, and community service) as primary catalysts in addiction recovery, criminal desistance, and larger changes in global health, quality of life and social contribution. In his new book, *Pathways to Recovery and Desistance: The Role of the Social Contagion of Hope*, Professor Best draws upon his community and prison research studies in Australia and the UK to explore this alternative approach and its programmatic and policy implications.

Addiction and criminal offending have been historically viewed primarily through the lens of personal pathology with remediation strategies focused primarily on intrapersonal interventions. What most distinguishes Professor Best's work is his placement of these behaviours within their ecological context. His suggestion that these behavioural aberrations are as much a function of pro-social disconnection as personal character or morality dramatically widens the scope of potential interventions. He asks that we see people not in terms of the complexity of their problems and needs, but in the range of their untapped capacities and possibilities. This shift in focus from deficits to assets is pregnant with possibilities. Few people have more articulately suggested that people who were once part of complex social and public health problems can be transformed into assets critical to the solution of these problems. The further suggestion that such transformation processes can be socially contagious at a community level is a particularly intriguing and promising idea. Put simply, Professor Best suggests that the journey from person against community (the 'I' orientation so common within addiction and criminal careers) to person within community (the 'We' orientation so pervasive within recovery narratives) has as much to do with the community environment as individual personality or character and that community environments can be shaped to initiate and speed such journeys.

Studies of interventions into compulsive drug use and criminal conduct have focused to a great extent on pathology reduction. Outcomes have been measured on the elimination or reduction of drug use or criminal conduct from an otherwise unchanged life, but few have evaluated what such interventions add to one's global health and quality of life in the community or how changes in personal health influence community health. Readers will discover that much of Best's work focuses on these latter benefits. His models of community intervention focus on additive and multiplicative effects of hope on individuals, families, social networks, key social institutions and whole communities.

Professor Best explores a series of catalytic ideas (such as recovery capital, the social identity model of recovery, recovery landscapes) and community level intervention strategies (for example, Asset Based Community Development) and offers case studies of action research testing these ideas and methods. Well-conceived and well-written, *Pathways to Recovery and Desistance* will find a most appreciative audience among policymakers, systems administrators, those working in direct service roles within addiction treatment and correctional roles, as well as the growing legions of people with lived recovery experience who are using that experience as a platform for policy advocacy, community revitalisation activities, and volunteer peer recovery support projects.

William L. White,
Emeritus Senior Research Consultant,
Chestnut Health Systems
Author, *Slaying the Dragon: The History of Addiction Treatment and Recovery in America*, *Let's Go Make Some History: Chronicles of the New Addiction Recovery Advocacy Movement*

1

What we know about recovery, desistance and reintegration

Overview

Pathways to Recovery and Desistance is an attempt to build on what we know about how people manage to reintegrate back into communities and society following prolonged careers of substance use and offending. There are a small and very fortunate group of people who get into trouble with the police or develop a problem with drugs or alcohol that manage to overcome those problems without external help, but that is not who this book is written about or for. The focus of this work is about how to support people who either had few skills, resources or supports to start with or who managed to lose them in the course of their using or offending careers.

This is a story of hope and how it can spring up in the most unlikely settings and circumstances. Each of the case studies described in the book should be a source of inspiration based on a vision for hope and change, and a sense of connectedness and hope. Many of these examples arose without any awareness of research background or theory, but I would like to think that all of them ultimately benefited from the lessons learned from theory and previous practice. There may well be nothing unique about the examples I have been involved in and have chosen, but they illustrate how social movements arise and can be charted and measured. My role has been to chronicle the blossoming of hope and its impact on blighted, marginalised and excluded lives.

Reviewing the literature

This first chapter provides an overview of the emerging research evidence on what recovery from substance use and desistance from offending mean, how often they are achieved and what we know about the things that can initiate and sustain positive changes. The literature review will contain an initial overview of what we know about recovery and desistance, an overview on recovery capital, and a focus on social and community capital in relation to addictions, and to restorative justice processes and therapeutic jurisprudence approaches in criminal justice. There is a lot of previous research material – drawn from a range of academic disciplines – but I will attempt to distil them down into clear findings and conclusions and will use them to build a story that forms the basis for the projects that are described in the subsequent chapters.

This will be embedded in a broader review of what the strengths-based literatures from psychology, criminology and criminal justice have contributed in research evidence and in the development of new conceptual models to our understanding of addressing exclusion and rehabilitation. This will be set against a social policy context of increasing engagement with a rehabilitative model and a recovery model, primarily from the UK, but also how these things have played out in Australia. This is a book about hope so it will all be written from a strengths-based perspective and most of this evidence is set in communities, although these communities vary markedly in their context and setting.

The final research and theory piece will look at the evidence around communities and community building, and how this has been used in the addictions and offending fields to improve theory and practice around reintegration. This will provide an overview of the conceptual model of community capital and its relationship to personal and social capital and will frame the approach for building a knowledge base from each of the case studies and examples. In each of the following sections, there will be a brief summary of the evidence followed by the conclusions and implications for building a model of reintegration based on connection and community capital.

Recovery definitions, theory and evidence

The primary definitions of recovery come from two main sources – consensus groups that were convened and reported in the US and then in the UK, both of which were chaired by the same eminent academic, Dr Tom McLellan. The Betty Ford Institute Consensus Group defines recovery from substance dependence as a 'voluntarily maintained lifestyle characterised by sobriety, personal health and citizenship' (2007: 222). This position is consistent with the UK Drug Policy Commission (2008: 6) statement on recovery as 'voluntarily sustained control over substance use which maximises health and wellbeing and participation in the rights, roles and responsibilities of society'. The key issue for both of these definitions is that they recognise that recovery is a process. In the Betty Ford document, recovery is actually split into three phases – 'early recovery' which represents the first year of recovery, 'sustained recovery' which is the period between one and five years into recovery, and 'stable recovery' which refers to the time beyond five years into recovery. The reason why this is seen as crucial is that the likelihood of relapse is estimated to reduce from around 50–70% in the first year to around 15% after five years of continuous recovery. Dennis et al (2014) have argued that it is after five years that recovery becomes self-sustaining, while prior to that point external supports are required. To a large extent, the science of recovery has focused on the processes and supports needed to help people reach five years of continuous recovery and what is needed additionally beyond this point.

However, before examining what predicts recovery and enables it to happen, it is worth briefly reviewing the evidence around the prevalence of recovery, with the strongest supporting evidence coming from a review for the US Substance Abuse and Mental Health Services Administration (SAMHSA) by Sheedy and Whitter (2009). They concluded that of all those who experience a lifetime substance dependence, 58% will achieve stable recovery. Although White's (2012) review of 415 papers reached a more conservative conclusion that just over half of those with a lifetime substance disorder will eventually achieve recovery and/or remission, both of these reviews provide an extremely positive rejoinder to those who interpret addiction as a chronic relapsing condition in an unnecessarily pessimistic light. People can and do recover, and the evidence would suggest that more than half of those who ever experience a substance addiction will ultimately lead a rich and fulfilling life beyond their substance use. This should in no way be taken to downplay the terrible toll on individuals, families and communities from addiction, or the appalling and often unnecessary loss of life.

However, it does provide impetus for a greater understanding of under what circumstances recovery is possible, and what are the characteristics of the individual and the setting that support and enable recovery to happen. And intimately linked to this is the question of what we can do to support this process. One of the key concepts in the recovery literature is around who we mean in this context by 'we'. In a recovery-oriented system of care (Sheedy and Whitter, 2009; Kelly and White, 2011), this is not simply down to professionals. While there may be a need for clinical interventions for many substance users (detoxification, rehabilitation, counselling, medication and so on), this is neither necessary nor sufficient, and recovery is something that happens in and is supported by the community. What this involves is a recognition that recovery may start with specialist clinical treatment, but it will always be sustained by efforts made in the lived community, long beyond the point of involvement of addiction professionals. As will be shown, there is a clear (and evidence-based) role for peer-based mutual aid and community groups, and for families and friends, ideally in partnership with a range of professionals and community groups and activities.

However, there is a second unique community quality to recovery which has recently been characterised as 'pre-figurative' (Beckwith et al, 2016). This challenges the above definitions as being too individualistic and suggests that recovery should be considered both to be a social phenomenon (as outlined in Best, 2014), but also as a 'movement'. According to this argument, recovery should be considered as something to belong to as well as a label of an internal state – people who attend recovery walks, visit recovery cafes and recovery support centres are active players within a community and a movement, and that sense of collectivism and solidarity itself offers hope and possibility.

This is part of a wider discussion of setting that will be presented below under social and community capital but it is worth emphasising that the switch from a medical to a recovery model is characterised in part from the idea that addiction and recovery are no longer considered to be things that happen inside a body to a model where the social and community spaces are seen as an essential and intrinsic part of the process, and which has an impact on the community in which it occurs.

So what do we know about who recovers and under what circumstances? The primary evidence around mechanisms presented here will be about social change factors. Moos (2007) reviewed the evidence on the psychological mechanisms underpinning recovery and concluded that there were two fundamental interpersonal processes – social learning in which role models provide an example of how to live recovery and 'social control' through which group members will learn and conform to the group's norms. In addition, opportunities for social learning by observing and imitating the recovery behaviours of more experienced peers in recovery promotes the two internalised changes – first the development of coping skills, and second, behavioural economics in which positive attitudes, beliefs and expectations that support sustained recovery come to dominate the individual's value system. The key conclusion from this review is that there are critical 'internal changes' in values, coping skills, and so on, but that these may need a range of social supports and guidance for them to flourish and mature.

Further evidence for the centrality of social processes in recovery is provided by Litt et al (2007, 2009). In this randomised controlled trial, people who completed residential detoxification from alcohol were randomly allocated to either standard aftercare or to a 'network support' intervention that involved developing a relationship with at least one non-drinking peer, which was called the 'network support' condition in the trial. Compared to standard aftercare, those who added at least one non-drinking member to their social network showed a 27% increase at 12 months post-treatment in the likelihood of treatment success (defined as being without alcohol 90% of the time). Similarly, Longabaugh et al (2010) found that greater opposition to a person's drinking from within their social network predicted more days without alcohol use both during and after treatment, and fewer heavy drinking days post-treatment. In addition, less frequent drinking within the person's social network predicted more days without alcohol use during and after treatment.

The change in social networks is important in part because it supports changes in how people see themselves – and the issue of identity has long been considered as central to recovery (as indeed it has been to desistance as will be outlined in the next section). Biernacki (1986: 141) argued that, in order to achieve recovery, 'addicts must fashion new identities, perspectives and social world involvements wherein the addict identity is excluded or dramatically depreciated'. In the UK context, McIntosh and McKeganey (2000, 2002) collected the recovery narratives of 70 former addicts in Glasgow, Scotland, and concluded that, through substance misuse, the addicts' 'identities have been seriously damaged by their addiction' (McIntosh and McKeganey, 2002: 152). On this basis, they argued that recovery required the restoration of a currently 'spoiled' identity. This argument however provoked a negative response on the grounds that individuals will often have multiple identities and Radcliffe (2011) used the example of motherhood as a positive identity that could assist in overcoming the addiction identity and enabling an initiation of recovery endeavours. For the substance user, discarding the addict identity, suffused as it is with stigmatising and excluding connotations, is not going to be straightforward because of both societal responses to addiction and because of the social binds the user may have to their using peers – who might include family members and close friends.

Therefore, contact with a recovery-oriented social network is important because it affords exposure to both recovery values and processes (Longabaugh et al, 2010; Moos, 2007), and the creation of a social environment in which an emerging sense of self as 'non-using' or 'in recovery' can be nurtured. Equally importantly, it allows the user to see that recovery is possible, that people who are in recovery can flourish and, just as importantly, many of them are keen to support people new to recovery in this process. This is where social support and social learning will merge to create an environment of hope and provide the scaffolding that enables the individual to develop the tools and the underlying commitment and motivation to support their recovery journey.

It will be apparent that I have said almost nothing so far about what treatment can do to support this process and what role professionals have in supporting the recovery process. One of the key findings has been around the key role that peers can play (White, 2009) and their role is largely community based but that does not mean there is not a central role for professionals, and much of this evidence has been focused on the idea of recovery-oriented systems of care. The principles for the implementation of a successful system have been outlined by the SAMHSA (Sheedy and Whitter, 2009), which also defined 17 elements of recovery-oriented systems of care and services:

1. Person-centred
2. Inclusive of family and other ally involvement
3. Individualised and comprehensive services across the lifespan
4. Systems anchored in the community
5. Continuity of care
6. Partnership–consultant relationships
7. Strength-based
8. Culturally responsive
9. Responsiveness to personal belief systems
10. Commitment to peer recovery support services
11. Integrated services
12. System-wide education and training
13. Inclusion of the voices and experiences of recovering individuals and their families
14. Ongoing monitoring and evaluation
15. Evidence driven
16. Research based
17. Adequately and flexibly funded

This model suggests a way of linking what is a personally driven approach to recovery as a process of choice and self-determination. Indeed there is an acronym that summarises the evidence of what works in the delivery of recovery programmes – CHIME – which stands for Connectedness; Hope; Identity; Meaning and Empowerment (Leamy et al, 2011). This approach will be central to the CHIME In Action model that will be used to summarise and conclude the findings in the studies that make up this book. Although this model was developed in the context of mental health recovery programmes, it is a good yardstick to assume that programmes that will support addiction recovery will result in positive social connections, the nurturing of a sense of hope that recovery is possible, a refined personal and social identity about hope and change, a sense of purpose and meaning and a feeling of self-determination and empowerment.

At this point, we will switch focus to a brief summary of what we know about desistance from offending. The desistance literature comes from a different academic tradition, but many of the themes are the same as are some of the same weaknesses around a lack of evidence about what constitutes effective professional practice, or how treatment systems (probation in particular) can be configured to support lasting change in offenders. The key ideas will be presented in the next section and then there will be a review of areas of similarity and difference.

Desistance definitions, theory and evidence

As with recovery, there have been debates about definitions, and a growing consensus that desistance from offending should be considered to be a process rather than a state. Maruna and Farrall (2004) have proposed that there are two distinct phases – primary desistance which refers to gaps in the offending career (or periods of non-offending) and secondary desistance as the gradual movement to a status, role and identity as a non-offender. However, McNeill (2014) has recently introduced the concept of 'tertiary desistance' to describe a sense of belonging to a community, and that desistance requires not only a change in identity but the corroboration of that new identity within a (moral) community. This concept will be examined further in later discussion around community capital but the key point is that desistance, like recovery, is not something that an individual can simply do for themselves – it requires the cooperation and at least tacit support of a number of other actors, some directly connected to the offender, and others less so. This is summarised in McNeill et al's (2005: 16) conclusion that

> desistance resides somewhere in the interfaces between developing personal maturity, changing social bonds associated with certain life transitions, and the individual subjective narrative constructions which offenders build around these key events and changes. It is not just the events and changes that matter; it is what these events and changes mean to the people involved.

The origins of desistance research are embedded within a tradition of life course criminology and what has often been referred to as the age-crime curve. Laws and Ward (2011: 30) summarise this evidence as '[t]here is a dramatic increase in criminal activity from age 7 to about 17, then a gradual trailing off until about age 45 when it begins the final decline to zero or near zero offences'. It has been assumed that this shift is a maturational process where individuals age out of crime although this neither explains why this happens nor why there should be individual variability in these changes. Thus, unlike with recovery, the assumption is that virtually every offender will eventually desist, and that the questions are really about why this happens, with splits in models between those that emphasise personal agency and those that focus more on social systems and structures. This is an age-old discussion about the extent to which behaviour is shaped by personal choice and decision making or by structures and processes that are beyond personal control, like the law or levels of social and financial inequality.

One of the key 'structural' theories is the 'informal social control' model advanced by Sampson and Laub (1992, 2003). By scrutinising the contextual factors around the age-crime relationship, Sampson and Laub identified pathways out of offending through attachment to stable employment, romantic and family relationships and the associated social status afforded to those persons transitioning from offending. Their research generated a new approach based on the mediating effects of informal social controls, social processes and social bonds. The significance of Laub and Sampson's work lay in their conclusion that desistance from crime was not linked to age per se, but was associated with life transitions which themselves are contingent on wider social variables such as changes in social status and with the expanding repertoire of life experiences. Further, in their later writings, Sampson and Laub (2003) used a more qualitative data approach that acknowledged the role of experience and personal interpretation of events. In a review of their life course model, Laub et al (2006: 281–2) assert that 'we recognise that both the social environment and the individuals are influenced by the interaction of structures and choice … In other words, we are always embedded in social structures'.

The work of Sampson and Laub is also credited with introducing aspects of identity change and individual agency into theories of desistance that had often been omitted from earlier desistance approaches (Paternoster and Bushway, 2009). This more psychological approach is evident in the work of both Giordano and Maruna. Giordano et al's symbolic interactionist approach to desistance stressed the significance of social processes, social interactions and socially derived emotions (Giordano et al, 2002). The focus is on *the other in desistance*, asserting that individuals do not desist alone. Giordano et al proposed a four-part 'theory of cognitive transformation' (2002: 999–1002), where emphasis is on understanding how one engages, in the first instance, (cognitively) with opportunities or 'hooks for change'. For Giordano there are basically four stages – first, a change in the offender's openness to change; second, exposure towards one or more hooks for change; third, the opportunity for the development of a 'replacement self'; and fourth, a transformation in the way that the offender views themselves and their situation. In other words, for Giordano, desistance is a process that involves psychological change that enables situational opportunities to be seized and this leads to lasting changes in identity and wellbeing, but where identity plays a crucial role.

The other key writer in the area of desistance theory is Shadd Maruna. In Maruna's (2001) Liverpool desistance study, based on interviews with 50 former or current offenders, 30 of whom were classified as desisting and 20 as persisting offenders, two distinct patterns emerged. Maruna argued that to desist from crime, ex-offenders needed to develop a coherent, pro-social identity that was characterised by a 'redemption script' in contrast to the stories of woe ('condemnation scripts') that were typical of the stories of persisting offenders. Maruna highlighted the significance of the self-narratives of the desisting cohort in his study as being care-oriented and other-centred, rather than focusing on *just* the individual (and their intimate social networks). Successful desistance is often signalled through engagement in socially visible generative activities: giving back earns a form of social redemption; engaging in visible pro-social activities, the enactment of redemption activities or roles that legitimise claims to a changed status (Maruna, 2012). This model reintroduces agency as a powerful force in shaping change, although Maruna's work can be seen as interactionist in that it also emphasises the importance of social experiences and opportunities.

So what are the implications of the desistance approach for interventions? There is a limited body of work in this area, particularly in the UK context. Rex (1999), studying offenders on probation in the UK, has highlighted desistance-focused officer–offender relationships as characterised by trust, emphasising the role of the worker as a therapeutic agent of change – with the author reporting that around half of all the study participants developed a positive relationship with their probation officer that generated feelings of trust and commitment. Similarly, Farrall's (2002) study of 199 probationers identified desistance as being closely related to the offender's motivation to change and to the social and personal support networks that supported these changes. Nonetheless, Farrall cautions that both probationers and their workers felt that success factors were generally beyond the scope of their working relationship, relating more to the motivation of the client and to social and contextual factors around things like employment and housing. For this reason, Farrall advocated for interventions to be directed more strongly towards the community and to be less focused on one-to-one intervention methods.

However, there is little in the way of organisational or systems research in the probation field in terms of what is required to support pathways to sustainable desistance. Thus, in both areas, there is an emerging evidence base about when and how people will typically achieve desistance and/or recovery, and a recognition of the importance of the broader context, yet limited empirical (or even conceptual) work done around the configuration of systems and services to support change. The next section will start to understand what factors make recovery more or less likely and the impact on desistance will also be discussed as a part of this process.

Social and recovery capital

There are two primary sources for models of social capital, one from France and one from the US. The French sociologist Pierre Bourdieu (1985) argued that social networks are a valuable asset and that interaction, a sense of belonging and the relationships of trust and tolerance that are subsequently developed are key resources particularly in communities where there is a lack of financial capital and the resulting limitations in access to resources. Social capital here includes the rich social networks, histories and cultures that afford a sense of belonging and meaning, and that provide resource and support to individuals and networks. For Putnam (2000), in the US context, social capital was characterised both as a resource that individuals can draw upon but also as a commitment to the group and reciprocity is central to his conceptualisation of social capital. In other words, social capital is a bind – a form of social connection that affords resources but also generates obligations through dynamic social interactions. Putnam (1995) also differentiated between 'bonding' capital (the strength of links within established groups) and 'bridging' capital which refers to the links and associations between groups and one of the key conclusions from Putnam is that individuals from marginalised communities can have strong bonds in their social networks but still have little access to community resources if there are not bridges to more connected and engaged groups. Thus, for adolescents involved in gangs or drug use for instance, the problem may not be about social isolation but rather is about their immersion in groups who are excluded and have no 'bridges' to more well connected groups or resources in the local community.

De Silva et al (2005) have suggested that there are five component parts to social capital:

1. the density of community and personal networks;
2. civic engagement and participation;
3. a sense of belonging in the community;
4. reciprocity and cooperation with fellow citizens; and
5. trust in the community.

What is more, there is emerging evidence that higher social capital is associated with lower rates of overdose mortality. In a US study assessing overdose rates at a county level, there was an inverse association between higher rates of social capital and overdose rates (Zoorob and Salemi, 2017). Although the authors accept limitations with the measures of social capital (the density of civic and non-profit organisations; percentage of adults who vote in a presidential election; response rate to the census; and number of tax-exempt non-profits in the county), 55% of low mortality counties were in the highest two quintiles of social capital. The same was true for less than 25% of high mortality counties. The authors suggest that one of the mechanisms through which this might work is through facilitating recovery, based on social connections and their capacity to provide access to social and material resources. What is clear from this study is that the connections available in communities have a significant effect on the wellbeing (and even the life chances) of vulnerable populations such as injecting drug users.

There has since been an explosion of academic work around the idea of social capital but a more recent concept is that of 'recovery capital' (Granfield and Cloud, 1999, 2009) based on many of the core concepts of social capital, and defined by Granfield and Cloud as 'the sum total of one's resources that can be brought to bear on the initiation and maintenance of substance misuse cessation' (Cloud and Granfield, 2009: 1972). This model has provided the foundation for examining key elements of recovery resources at the intra- and interpersonal levels as well as the community resources required (Best and Laudet, 2010) and has provided the foundations for attempting to map and measure recovery wellbeing and progress (for example Groshkova et al, 2012). Best and Laudet outlined three key components of recovery capital:

- *Personal recovery capital* refers to the personal skills, capabilities and resources the individual possesses. The key resources are likely to include self-esteem, self-efficacy, communication skills, coping skills and resilience.
- *Social recovery capital* refers to the social supports the individual can draw upon to support their recovery journey, but, as Putnam (2000) has argued, it is the strength of the individual's bind to these positive networks that is critical in defining social recovery capital. As will be outlined, it is also essential that the person moves away from social groups and networks that are associated with substance use and the related lifestyle, which is often easier said than done, because that may include family members, lifelong friends, their partner and the parents of their children.
- *Community recovery capital* refers to the contextual factors of recovery in two senses. In the first sense, it is about opportunities to access houses that are safe in neighbourhoods that the person can engage with and that provide opportunities for training and employment. The second type of community recovery capital is specific to addiction and refers to the pathways to recovery support. This includes high quality and evidence-based specialist addiction treatment but also involves the availability of community recovery support groups and viable and strong connections between specialist treatment and the opportunity for continuity of care in the community. In this context, the community can provide both the pull to recovery that William White speaks of in the foreword to this book and to the resources that the community can offer to support the journey to enduring change.

The conclusion that Best and DeAlwis (2017) reached was that, in the same way that recovery is a journey that typically takes place over years, so is the accrual of recovery capital. Dennis et al (2014) have argued that the five years that is regarded as the typical period for progressing from early to stable recovery is in effect the transition from reliance on external help to self-sustaining recovery, and that much of that help comes from social and community capital. Best and DeAlwis make a similar case for recovery capital growth in arguing that supports from both social networks and from broader community structures are essential as 'scaffolding' around the person in early recovery that affords them the space and time to develop the internal qualities to sustain their own recovery. In this sense, it is social recovery capital that is seen as the trigger for building personal skills and resources to support ongoing and stable recovery, but that this takes place in a community that can either support or block the growth of personal recovery capital.

Cloud and Granfield (2009) have extended the debate on recovery capital by arguing that there are not only assets and strengths but also 'negative recovery capital' that constitutes a range of barriers to recovery change. Cloud and Granfield identify four such barriers – suggesting that the evidence would indicate that the recovery journey is more difficult for those with histories of mental health problems, with significant histories of involvement with the criminal justice system, for people who are older and, more contentiously, for women.

While there are problems with conceptualising 'negative assets', particularly within a framework that focuses on strengths and positive factors, the issue of women's experiences of recovery and desistance are important here. Why should Cloud and Granfield have identified being female as a barrier to recovery? The answer is at least in part about how society responds to addiction – with women more likely to face exclusion and stigmatisation than their male counterparts, based on greater social disapproval of female addiction and its consequences. Here the concept of 'negative recovery capital' is useful if framed in the context of societal responses where stigma and discrimination may well constitute significant barriers to change.

Indeed, in the literature on desistance, McNeill (2014) has introduced the concept of 'tertiary desistance' to describe a sense of belonging to a community, arguing that desistance requires not only a change in identity, a change in social networks and their response to the offender, but also the corroboration of that new identity within a (moral) community. In other words, desistance and recovery cannot be achieved by the endeavours of the primary actor alone. They can stop offending and stop using, they can change their social networks and belief systems, but only external partners (individuals, groups and organisations) can afford the opportunity for full reintegration through acceptance of the individual. It is at this point that I must introduce the idea of recovery as a 'social contract' embedded firmly in the principles of social justice. While many individuals will be able to motivate themselves and will turn their lives around against all kinds of adversity, in itself a remarkable achievement, the reality is that stable and sustainable reintegration is not a personal decision or choice, but a complex process that involves the person making these changes, their families, their friends and their neighbours. But it also involves college enrolment officers, potential employers, and housing officials, who can provide hope or generate barriers. Of course, this is not only the decision of individual officials, but will reflect legislation, policy, culture and other structural factors, yet it remains core to a model of social contagion that it is not simply a contagion restricted to those attempting the recovery journey or those who have been successful in it. This is a community process, and it is to the community we now turn to understand how some of these 'structural' factors may be influenced by community engagement processes.

Community capital and Asset Based Community Development

The first piece of research evidence I will draw on here is a remarkable body of work collectively known as the Framingham Heart Study and summarised in the book, *Connected* (Christakis and Fowler, 2009). This book summarises a series of public health studies that follow a cohort of adults from one US city over time in examining the spread of a range of health conditions (such as heart disease), public health matters (such as binge drinking and smoking) and broader lifestyle issues (such as divorce), and what predicts changes in these human experiences. The authors analysed data from health screens, in-depth health assessments and social network assessments at repeated time points to assess the impact of social networks on a diverse range of behaviours. And the results were startling – for health behaviours such as heart disease and obesity, there was a clear social effect, with the paper on obesity written up in the prestigious *New England Journal of Medicine*.

What the authors showed was that social rather than geographic proximity predicted elevated risk or protection (depending on the behaviour assessed). If your friend became obese, your likelihood of becoming obese at the next survey had just increased dramatically, and the same effect held, to varying degrees, for a diverse range of behaviours. These behaviours included divorce, where a similar contagion effect was reported, clearly indicating that there does not need to be an underlying biological component to social contagion. What Christakis and Fowler (2009) demonstrated was that it is not only 'negative' behaviours like obesity and binge drinking that can spread through social contagion, but also positive behaviours like smoking cessation. While it was the case that the contagion effect was stronger for closer relationships, the 'ripple' effect of social contagion was much more pervasive, so that there was a significant effect at up to three degrees of separation. In other words, behaviour was contagious not only through friends, but also through friends of friends, and even through friends of friends of friends.

Why is this important in a book on recovery from substance use and desistance from offending? What the Framingham Heart Study shows is that social networks can shape behaviour and that both positive and negative behaviours can proliferate in this way, and also that change is a continuous dynamic of multiple social influences. For this to happen, people have to have social exposure to the behaviour – in other words, if healthy behaviours like eating vegetables or riding a bike are only spread among the middle classes, then the public health benefits will not reach the most vulnerable groups. It is also why it is important to ensure that champions of positive community engagement and belonging are made accessible and available to all of the members of a community whenever possible. All of this is only possible for people who are connected and so are open to the contagion effects that spread through networks.

As we move into the last piece of the academic jigsaw, which is around Asset Based Community Development (ABCD), the aim is to frame this in the context of an inclusive community whose assets are made available to vulnerable and excluded groups to improve those communities and to enact principles of social justice and fairness. ABCD (Kretzmann and McKnight, 1993) is a strengths-based model designed to identify and mobilise the indigenous resources that exist within even the most beleaguered communities – the people who make things happen, the informal groups and associations that offer a sense of pride and purpose, and the physical resources and assets that are available in the community, such as churches, libraries and schools that can provide meeting spaces and a diverse range of other resources. In many respects, the assets identified in ABCD are community capital and the aim of the model is to mobilise these to promote community engagement and wellbeing.

Kretzmann and McKnight (1993) set out to challenge the model where professionals were needed to solve the problems of communities. They were concerned that community problems were addressed by bringing in yet more professionals who compounded the problems and left communities even more depleted when they went home at night, and who had little or no personal stake in the communities they worked in. The ABCD model is in essence an attempt to coalesce local resources and to mobilise them for the benefit of communities. However, as McKnight and Block (2010) have argued, the identification of assets is only the starting point and there is a key group of individuals, called community connectors, required to mobilise the assets identified. This model has gained considerable traction in community development and recovery programmes in the UK, although the research evidence base remains limited, and concerns have been expressed that this is simply a cheap option in which the work of professionals is replaced by that of peers and communities. There is a further concern that what this means is that vulnerable populations simply absorb the resources of a community and that these can rapidly become depleted.

For this reason, a 'reciprocal community development' model was developed and piloted by the Salvation Army Eastern Division in Australia, building on the ideas of ABCD but with a clear emphasis of community building as a core part of the model (Best et al, 2014a). This was an initiative undertaken with two therapeutic communities (TCs) on the central coast of

Australia designed to create 'communities without walls' and that enabled the local communities to utilise the resources available at the TC and for residents of the TC to build their community connections and bridging social capital by becoming active in the local community, rather than remaining secluded and cloistered in the treatment setting. The aim was very clearly reciprocal – for the TC (staff, volunteers and residents) to contribute to the wellbeing and cohesion of the local community and, in doing so, to benefit the recovery journey of the residents of the TC. With former residents and staff members acting as community connectors, a much stronger bond was forged with the local community and clearer pathways for residents to develop networks and skills in the community were established, as described in Chapter 2. The aim was to create benefit to the community and benefit to the clients with a residual effect of a stronger and more connected community with greater engagement and inclusion of vulnerable communities.

Overall, the purpose of the ABCD model, as described here, is about mobilising community capital and making it accessible to people early in recovery who do not possess the connections or the resources that can provide the support and assistance they will need. How this fits into the overall model that is tested and outlined in the book is summarised in the following section.

Conclusions: an integrated model of hope contagion

There is a growing body of research that supports the idea that pathways to both recovery and desistance are complex processes that take years to complete and that require not only huge personal commitment and motivation, but the support and participation of a diverse range of other people. Those external partners to recovery include family and friends, partners and neighbours, but also include that much more diverse and less visible group of professionals, and the organisations and values those professionals represent, which is why theories of recovery and desistance involve both social networks and wider societal structures.

While it is clear that to achieve stable desistance and recovery can take many years (and for some people numerous attempts), motivation and commitment are not enough and as Dennis and colleagues (2014) have argued, the time to stable recovery is around five years and is characterised by a transition from the need for external support in the early months to one of self-determination and self-sustaining recovery after around five years of sober time. The assumption made in this book follows from that timeline as it would appear that, for most marginalised and excluded people who have suffered from addiction or involvement in offending or the criminal justice system, it is a long and slow process to build up the coping skills, resilience skills and the self-esteem and self-efficacy to allow the levels of self-determination and ability to cope with adversity necessary to deal with life's challenges to develop.

It is also likely that in the course of their offending or using careers, most offenders and problem drug users will have either never had much in the way of positive social or community capital to start with, or will have used up the goodwill and support of those who could have supported their pathway to recovery. Further, as addiction and offending have become lifestyle choices, their networks will increasingly have been populated by people who are also marginalised and excluded. Thus, for any model or system that is designed to support recovery, one of the main challenges is how to ensure that desistance and recovery is a sufficiently attractive option that individuals will be engaged and motivated to make the effort to change and that they will receive the support and opportunities they need to sustain it.

In this respect, the solution may lie in the idea of recovery capital, and particularly in the dynamic relationship between components of recovery capital, with the assumption this book is based on building sustainable personal capital necessarily involves strong social capital and through this capital access to resources and opportunities in local communities. As Weaver (2016) has argued, this is a dynamic process in which the person must come to see opportunities as real and meaningful and through reflexive process see themselves as a different person with a different relationship to their networks and their community, and a different set of values and beliefs that relate to their ability to solve problems and to cope with life challenges.

The focus of the book is a very practical one: it is about what we can learn about and from communities that have managed to mobilise resources to support the reintegration attempts of people with substance use or offending issues. The key research questions that the book will attempt to address are about what kinds of resources are potentially available, how they can be mobilised, and what kind of people make effective community connectors (and what supports do they need to do this).

We know, particularly from the recovery evidence base, that it is typically around five years before people achieve stable recovery that they can sustain themselves (Betty Ford Institute Consensus Group, 2007; Dennis et al, 2014). This means that there is a five-year window where people recovering do not typically have the personal recovery capital to sustain their own recovery without external supports, although the level of support needed is likely to diminish across this time period, as we have shown in the various Life in Recovery studies undertaken in the UK and Australia (Best, 2015; Best et al, 2015a). We also know that the social networks they will need are often not accessible in early recovery and a transition in social networks will be needed to provide the necessary guidance and motivation (Best et al, 2016; Longabaugh et al, 2010).

So what is presented in the chapters that follow are a series of pilot projects that I have had the good fortune to be involved in which have tested core aspects of this model and which have attempted to identify, mobilise and coordinate community resources and to utilise those resources to assist people with offending and substance use issues reintegrate through accessing social and community recovery capital. The cases presented here are by no means unique but they represent a personal journey for me that has been full of excitement, and hope, and inspiration, and that characterise the power and potential of local communities to support and reintegrate vulnerable and marginalised communities and populations. This is firmly embedded within a strengths-based model which has three primary goals:

- improving the wellbeing and connectedness of the client;
- improving the wellbeing and connectedness of the connector or worker; and
- improving the cohesion and connectedness of the community in which the project takes place.

The positive component of all of the projects featured in this book is in part manifest as they all generated not only a contagion of recovery but also a contagion of hope that influences all of those who have a meaningful stake in the process. They all represent alliances between professionals and peers; between diverse stakeholders in each community and through doing this generating new connections and new community resources. This model of working needs a lot more research and evaluation but the process is in itself generative and creative and positive and this will be shown through the richness of the cases discussed.

Key lessons

- Recovery and desistance have many common characteristics: they are processes that take place over time and involve changes in social networks and opportunities for reintegration at a community level.
- Recovery and desistance both typically involve changes in identity and a sense of hope, connection, meaning and empowerment.
- At the start of the recovery journey, many people lack supportive social networks and access to resources in the community, either through processes of marginalisation or exclusion or as a result of their using and offending careers.
- Communities contain many different resources and assets, but for a variety of reasons many of these are not accessible to people early in recovery or desistance.
- ABCD is a model for identifying, mobilising and integrating resources in communities and can be used as a part of reintegration efforts through creating pathways supported by community connectors.
- The overall aim of the book is to demonstrate that community engagement is a key strategy in supporting the long-term reintegration of people attempting to reintegrate into the community.

2

Australian origins: building bridges and community connections

The aim of this chapter is to explore the power of community engagement for both desistance and recovery based on two Australian case studies. These case studies show the extent of assets that exist in the community and the multiple methods through which such resources can be mobilised to support the reintegration of excluded and vulnerable populations. As part of a personal journey, these two very different examples inspired me to work more in this area and to understand that community engagement and community development are central to establishing sustainable platforms for reintegration and rehabilitation. Following a brief overview of the literature that will focus on the principles of ABCD and its impact on communities, the two case studies will be presented and their implications for both method and the underlying conceptual model will be discussed.

Introduction: assets for recovery and therapeutic landscapes

In the UK, the highly influential Marmot Review (Marmot et al, 2010) argued that, in order to address health inequalities and to meet the needs of disadvantaged and excluded groups, much greater emphasis should be placed on supporting the growth and development of sustainable and inclusive communities. Similarly, using the concept of capital, Flora and Flora (2013) spoke of a 'seven capitals model' that was successful in supporting healthy and sustainable communities. They suggested that communities that were successful in developing healthy and sustainable communities focused on natural capital (such as access to green spaces); cultural capital (the richness of local traditions and activities); human capital (such as skills and education); social capital (not only in terms of bonding capital but also bridges to new groups and links to other strata of the community, including professional groups); political capital (in terms of access to decision making); financial capital (as traditional economic resources) and built capital (including access to amenities and physical resources). This model feeds into the idea of assets as currency but a currency that is complex in its origins and dynamism.

ABCD (Kretzmann and McKnight, 1993) offers a highly pragmatic and engaging approach to community development in which it is assumed that the most important resources in a local community are its people, informal groups and formal organisations, all of which represent community (and cultural) capital. Kretzmann and McKnight's model relies on unleashing the capacities of individuals within a community based on the assumption that everybody has capacities, abilities and gifts, and that the key task of the ABCD process is to release these through the human and cultural resources in the community. Thus, they argue that 'Each time a person uses his or her capacity, the community is stronger and the person more powerful. That is why strong communities are basically places where the capacities of local residents are identified, valued and used' (Kretzmann and McKnight, 1993: 13). They go on to argue that the key to the effectiveness of ABCD, as a strengths-based approach, is that it switches the perception of clients as having deficits and needs, to having capacities and gifts.

Kretzmann and McKnight (1993) therefore see the basis of their model as one in which the basic methodological building block is the initial creation of an inventory of the capacity of its residents. The seminal text they wrote in this area (*Building Communities from the Inside Out*, 1993) is effectively a guide on how to measure and mobilise community assets. They argue that once assets have been mapped, the second crucial task is around building strong relationships among the community's assets. Their fundamental model rests on the assumption that communities become stronger every time local residents become more connected for problem solving purposes, especially when those connections involve previously excluded individuals and groups. Beyond these individual stages of asset mapping and building connections, one of the primary objectives of the ABCD model is mobilising community assets for two purposes – economic development and for information sharing. It is also worth noting that the authors, for all their focus on community autonomy, do include a step that is around leveraging external resources to support locally driven developments. This is crucial as the model is not exclusively about communities being autonomous but also about building partnerships that support community development and growth, including those with outside and professional bodies. The focus in this book will be on that idea of a coalition of professionals, communities and marginalised groups for the benefit of all, and which will generate further assets and resources in the community.

While the initial tasks are around identifying assets and building partnerships, there is a further human component to this process that involves identifying and engaging individuals who can support this process. These individuals are called 'community connectors' and are the focus of further work from the same group. McKnight and Block (2010) have argued that building integrated and supportive communities rests on 'more individual connections and more associational connections' (McKnight and Block, 2010: 132), which in turn relies on identifying those who have the capacity to connect others in our communities. They are effectively the contagion for activities and hope within communities and their active participation in a connections model is essential to both the likelihood and the speed of the spread of hope.

John McKnight (1995) identified two core characteristics of community connectors. The first of these rests on their abilities to identify assets – they are 'people with a special eye for the gift, the potential, the interest, the skills, the smile, the capacity of those who are said to be "in special need". Focusing upon these strengths, they introduce people into community life' (McKnight, 1995: 120). However, there is also a second quality, 'A second attribute of most, if not all, effective guides is that they are well connected in the inter-relationships of community life' (McKnight, 1995: 120). In other words, the connectors are the people with the vision to see both potential and positives and also in a position to mobilise these assets through their connections.

Although it is a model about communities and processes, it is an inherently social approach, which places great faith and emphasis on individuals and their ability and willingness to commit to actions and activities for the benefit of their neighbourhood and what they perceive to be their communities. McKnight and Block (2010) refer to such people as community connectors, and they argue that, to make more accepting and integrated communities, 'we want to make more visible people who have this connecting capacity. We also want to encourage each of us to discover the connecting possibility in our own selves' (McKnight and Block, 2010: 132). The key message from this work is that the aim of the project is both to afford opportunities for people who are marginalised and excluded to get involved in growing recovery capital, but in the process of doing so to build resources and assets in the community. Thus, the idea is to generate a therapeutic landscape for recovery in which place is central to the community capital component of recovery capital.

The concept of 'therapeutic landscapes' is described as "changing places, settings, situations, locales and milieus that encompass the physical, psychological and social environments associated with treatment or healing" (Williams, 1999: 2). This has been applied to recovery from alcohol and drugs and emphasises the importance of context in recovery. Wilton and DeVerteuil (2006) describe a cluster of alcohol and drug treatment services in San Pedro, California as a 'recovery landscape' in that it acts as a foundation of spaces and activities that promote recovery. Alcoholics Anonymous (AA) programmes provide ongoing support to people in recovery in San Pedro, but there are public actions to promote recovery as well. In San Pedro, for one day a year, all of those in recovery wear red shirts and there is an annual public recovery rally at which around 300 people participate in a recovery celebration event. This challenges stereotypes and stigma as 'program advocates positioned themselves and their program in opposition to other groups who were unable to strive for norms of responsibility and productivity' (Wilton and DeVerteuil, 2006: 659). Additionally, there is a day every year when everyone in the town wears a blue t-shirt to show their solidarity with the recovery movement and there is a series of events to both proclaim and celebrate the individual achievement of recovery but also to celebrate the role of the town in championing and supporting recovery pathways. By doing so, stigma and exclusion are challenged and hope is disseminated through a celebration of success and through high visibility of recovery success.

Overview of the two case studies in the chapter

The two case studies that follow are both examples of how this process plays out in practice. Both of these studies were opportunistic and were based on individuals or services that were strongly committed to partnership, client wellbeing and community engagement. In other words, there was already a commitment to some of the values that were relevant to ABCD. Indeed, the latter example attempts to extend this model by making an explicit variant that focuses specifically on reciprocity and the power of the idea of 'giving back' and embodying citizenship.

Dandenong Magistrates Court and ABCD to address repeat substance-related offending

The first case study looks specifically at the criminal justice system and a perennial problem of young people who were arrested for low level offending. Based on a therapeutic jurisprudence model (Wexler, 1999), two magistrates from the court in Dandenong (an outer suburban area of Melbourne, Victoria, with high levels of deprivation) engaged with me while I was working at Turning Point (a Victorian alcohol, drug and behavioural addiction research and treatment centre) to develop a model for continuity of care for offenders with substance use histories who were completing their sentences. The reason for the initial contact was a concern that there were a cohort of repeat offenders who seemed impervious to traditional forms of punishment and rehabilitation, and the aim was to identify alternative and more imaginative options for this group of young substance users who were getting into trouble with the law.

The rationale for the initiative was to pilot a project that would involve diversion from the criminal justice system through providing alternative activities that would offer hope to offenders and would create the possibility of a lasting change from substance use and offending. This was to be achieved by identifying assets in the local community and creating viable pathways into those assets using an assertive linkage approach. In this way, the local community was a key stakeholder in the success of the project.

The aim of the community linkage project was to identify appropriate community connectors to build bridges to community assets, with this group drawn from three primary pools: substance using offenders in the community, professionals working in relevant services and other members of the community – all of whom had skills and capabilities that would allow them to act as 'bridges' between offenders and community groups, such as AA, sporting clubs and other groups.

This approach is underpinned by an asset based model of community development which attempts to utilise strengths and resources that already exist in the community to achieve sustainable change. In this case the change we are referring to includes: 1) supporting offenders' own changes in substance use and offending behaviour at the individual level; and 2) promoting communities that are welcoming and supportive of recovery as opposed to communities that stigmatise and marginalise people with substance use problems and offending histories. This last part is central to the project and the models presented throughout this book are all predicated on the idea that community linkage has to be a positive sum game. This means that, in both the medium and long term, there have to be benefits for the community as well as for the individual. The underlying notions of social justice are discussed throughout the book, with the aim of community growth and connections based on inclusion and challenging stigma.

Setting and design

Dandenong is a suburb 30km south-east of Melbourne, in the Australian state of Victoria. The Greater Dandenong area has a population of just over 135,000 and has a greater proportion of people born overseas compared to Victorian and Australian averages (Australian Bureau of Statistics, 2013). Greater Dandenong also has a higher unemployment rate and lower median income as compared to Victorian and national averages (Australian Bureau of Statistics, 2013), and has a higher crime rate than the Victorian average (Community Indicators Victoria, 2013). It is also an area of considerable ethnic and cultural diversity with high rates of population transition, and so provides a challenge for people self-identifying as members of the community.

As the court was the starting point for the initiative, the aim was to assess what the characteristics of the target group were and what resources were available that they could be linked into. The initial pilot work involved a series of court observations undertaken by a member of the research team which occurred alongside a process of mapping community groups in the Dandenong area. This examined whether we could identify offenders who might benefit from the community linkage programme, and explored whether there were sufficient groups in the community to which offenders could be linked. This was all done in an exploratory and iterative way to adapt the established methodology to the local context and so that we were able to pick up local opportunities that arose. The initial phase also involved generating interest and engagement in the project from within the local community.

The key starting point was the two magistrates who were the drivers for the project – Greg and Pauline. In essence, their commitment to the reintegration of repeat offenders and their belief in the potential for regeneration was in effect the first asset that we mobilised. They became integral members of the project team and they were also able to help in two other ways. First, they acted as senior figures within a physical asset – as judges in the court system, they were able to commandeer parts of the building for use as a part of the process. Dandenong

Magistrates Court was already used as a kind of 'market place' for local services and agencies, and this had helped to create a sense in which the court building was a community resource that could be mobilised for events and activities and which represented a visual hub for the project. Thus, one of the successes of the model was that the Magistrates Court was used to host afternoon teas to bring together local stakeholders and potential community connectors, and the court building itself was transformed into a place for meeting and for hope. This mobilised an asset that would previously been associated with negative experiences for the target group involved in the project.

Second, both of our magistrates had worked there for some time and were well known and well respected figures in the local community. The starting point for establishing a network of connectors therefore started with them – their address books combined with their commitment to the project meant that they were our initial champions and their energy and enthusiasm was the starting point not only for a social contagion of hope but also for a social contagion of engagement and enthusiasm. The project team quickly learned that these are critical assets in developing and mobilising community resources.

It is also worth noting that in doing so, we were moving away from the original model outlined for ABCD by Kretzmann and McKnight. Neither of the magistrates lived in the area (and both would be classed as 'professionals') yet both were highly committed to the client group they worked with and to the idea of partnerships between professionals and community members and community groups. Central to the asset engagement model outlined in this book is the notion that there needs to be a balanced coalition between a range of professionals and a range of community stakeholders and that neither will be sufficient in their own rights. In essence, what we are proposing for working with vulnerable populations is a four-point coalition:

1. The target vulnerable group
2. Their families, partners and friends
3. Professionals and services
4. A diverse group of other members of the local community

The shared skills and resources of each of these groups bring with them different forms of social and community capital (Best and Laudet, 2010) that can create a broader range of skills and capabilities that can create support and learning opportunities for the marginalised and excluded population. However, the other key reason for including a professional group is to maximise the number of doors that are open and accessible and available to support the recovery pathway and journey.

Preliminary findings: suitability of the client group

Observations of public court proceedings to record substance use involvement were completed by one member of the research team as a means of identifying potential participants in the project. This involved observing court proceedings from the public gallery on four different days and collecting data on the characteristics of offenders and particularly where there were clear indications of substance use problems, and repeat appearances before the court. The court proceedings observed were a mixture of bail and bail review hearings, judicial monitoring, suspended sentence and breach of order hearings, as well as guilty plea hearings. Substance use was mentioned in just over a quarter (n=19, 27.9%) of the 68 cases observed, with alcohol, amphetamine type stimulants, and cannabis being the most commonly mentioned substances.

In most of these cases, substance use was considered to be a major underlying reason for offending. This means that around one in four cases at the Dandenong Magistrates' Court might benefit from the proposed community linkage programme, indicating the feasibility of the research project. Eleven of the individuals involved in court hearings where substance use was mentioned (except one) were male, the average age was 36 years (SD=10.4), and all had prior criminal histories. Whatever prior criminal justice responses they had received had not been a deterrent to further offending, reinforcing the need for innovative responses, and the need to develop interventions that provided the opportunity for sustainable change.

Past use of substance use treatment services was mentioned in under half of the cases (n=8, 42.1%), although 55.6% of people (n=10) were currently engaged in some form of treatment, and in 72.2% (n=13) of cases a recommendation for treatment was provided by the magistrate. What this would suggest is that specialist addiction treatment alone had not been sufficient to address their ongoing needs and that some additional form of support was required to break the cycle of substance use and offending, as the magistrates had suggested.

The focus on a therapeutic jurisprudence model at the Dandenong Magistrates Court was also borne out in sentencing/ recommendations, where the most common outcome was a community corrections order (CCO) (50%) followed by bail (12.5%) and deferred sentence (12.5%). Imprisonment was rare in instances where substance use was involved and was limited to one case only. Family members or friends were present in only one of the 19 cases where substance use was mentioned, suggesting that this group of offenders may lack immediate social capital and might benefit from engagement in community groups, further supporting the rationale and premise on which the connectedness intervention was based.

Available and accessible community assets

Having identified a need for community linkage and a lack of adequate social support in their indigenous social networks, our next task was to map community assets in the Dandenong region to understand the community groups to which offenders could potentially be linked. A number of formal health and welfare services exist in Dandenong and case managers were already working with people who are involved in the criminal justice system to facilitate access to these. While health and welfare services are important (and are indeed community assets), they do not always facilitate connections to broader community activities and less formal groups and supports. Our interest was therefore in mapping peer-led and informal groups in the community so that they could be embedded with and coordinated across specialist services.

We did this by searching online community directories and talking to magistrates in Dandenong, and by following up the leads that arose from those initial contacts. We identified

97 informal community groups in Dandenong and the diversity and scope of these is illustrated in Figure 2.1 below. The majority of groups identified were either sporting clubs (47.4%, n=46) or recreation groups (33.0%, n=32), such as fishing clubs and community bands. Training and support groups, which were often attached to formal services, included regular group programmes on community gardening, cooking, computers, art and craft and other similar activities, and these accounted for 9.3% (n=9) of groups. Importantly, there were also ten (10.3%) addiction recovery groups identified in the community. These provided peer support and mutual aid for people with substance use and mental health issues, including groups like AA and SMART Recovery (a mutual aid group based on the principles of cognitive behavioural therapy, run on a peer basis without the involvement of addiction professionals).

Recovery groups are likely to have the most experience of, and be the most welcoming to, people who are either currently or previously involved in the criminal justice system. These may be ideal targets for community linkage initially, and indeed there is a literature around assertive linkage to mutual aid groups (for example, Manning et al, 2012), but they may not be sufficient for all individuals and across all stages of the recovery journey. As

Figure 2.1: Community asset map of community groups (n=97) in Dandenong, Victoria

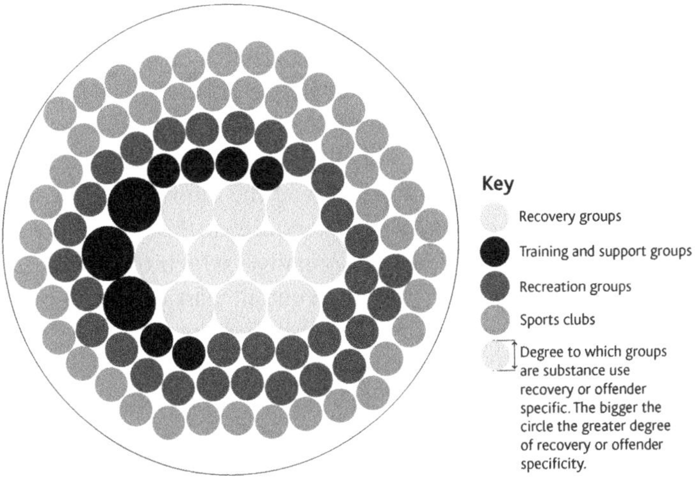

people's confidence, social networks and ability to participate in diverse group situations grows, there are a wide range of non-recovery specific groups available in Dandenong that can be accessed. The initial phase of the work was around identifying appropriate groups and then working out how to manage effective linkage into them, with the goal of addressing broad and holistic needs and interests across this population.

Thus, in the figure, the size of the dot is related to the extent to which the group is specifically designed to meet the needs of substance users and the colour of the dot designates what domain or area the group is in – they are not related to a geo-spatial mapping of groups in Dandenong. The groups were also a mixture of structured groups, some linked to specialist services, and informal community groups and associations that were more localised and run by volunteers and community members.

The next steps in this project involved the identification and recruitment of community connectors whose job it was to make this link, and to act as the bridge between the court and the offender on the one hand, and the community groups on the other. The connectors group were recruited from a combination of professionals, peers in recovery and members of the local community, overseen by a coordinating committee, akin to the process I had previously used with the recovery community in Barnsley, Yorkshire, in England (Best et al, 2013).[1]

However, at this point in the story we encountered resourcing issues with the project – the student who was working on the project completed his placement and we were unable to secure additional research funding to replace him or to fund training initiatives in the Magistrates Court. The project team continued to support our two magistrates, Greg and Pauline, but from this point on, the model became informally managed and without research support. Therefore, at this stage we will switch the focus to the second initiative, which took place in a therapeutic community on the central coast of New South Wales, in partnership with the Salvation Army, or, as they are known commonly in Australia, 'the Salvos'.

However, the key lessons learned from the project in Dandenong were around the possibility of generating community engagement in a project to include marginalised young people with almost no resource and in an incredibly short period of time. The downside of this is that it meant there was almost no sustainability to the initiative and establishing mechanisms for continuity was going to be important moving forward. The Dandenong project did not end at this point, but the initial thrust was not sustained and this has worrying implications for community trust and ongoing engagement that are explored in the later discussion of other projects.

Picking up the baton: Dooralong and reciprocal community development

In contrast to the complex urban mobility and deprivation of Dandenong, Dooralong is an idyllic setting. It is the rural setting for a 110-bedded residential rehabilitation service run by the Salvation Army in Queensland in Australia, which offers a therapeutic community intervention (DeLeon, 2000) to substance users with entrenched substance use history (many of whom have co-occurring offending and mental health histories). The Dooralong Transformation Centre opened not long before the start of the our project and is set in a large estate of 350 acres with extensive opportunities for sport as well as a broad range of therapeutic activities, and was part of a transition to a recovery-oriented approach to addiction treatment in the Salvation Army services in Australia.

The Transformation Centre represents not only a potential hub for recovery activity, but is also an asset for the community, containing in its grounds a large lake, stables and horses, and a range of sports and leisure options. Such a centre moves from a model of asset mobilisation to one of asset provision and so can be more appropriately be referred to as a reciprocal community development model, where the aim is not only to help the clients of the centre to access existing connectors and resources in the community but to ensure that the centre, its staff and clients also take on the role of providing assets to the wider community and playing an active role in engaging with and improving community life. Although Dooralong is a beautiful setting, it is isolated and has significant pockets of rural poverty and the managers of the centre could see the possibility of developing an alternative approach to delivering a TC, which they referred to as a 'TC without walls' (Best et al, 2014c).

The use of the centre, its staff and residents as community assets is part of an attempt at not only asset development but also building proximity and linkage between the treatment centre and the community, and, through doing this, challenging discriminatory practices and beliefs. This is the first initiative in which I started to form the idea of bridges as key to linking assets in one setting to the wider community in which it is embedded. Central to this idea was the determination of the director of clinical services at the Transformation Centre, Gerard Byrne, that the Salvation Army would run TCs 'without walls' and that they would be an active and contributing part of the communities in which they were based.

The explicit aim of the pilot project at Dooralong was to build a partnership with the Salvation Army to identify community connectors from within the TC and to utilise this initial cohort to actively engage the wider community in recovery-oriented activities including those associated with challenging stigma and discrimination. The intention was to attempt to move from an inward-looking model of recovery to one that more actively engaged the community and which attempted to create greater bridging capital to supplement the existing bonding capital among residents (Putnam, 2000). In other words, while it is well established that TC residents form strong relationships with fellow residents and with the staff, there is much less emphasis on external bonds that will be critical on their return to the community. Although all TCs have a 're-entry' phase towards the end of the period of residence, it is not clear how effectively that works in supporting long-term reintegration.

The adaptation of community connections that was used in the Dooralong project was based on four connected concepts:

- *Recovery Capital:* The sum of personal, social and community resources that an individual can draw on to support them in their recovery journey. It is fundamental to this work that recovery capital is seen as fluid – it can grow but it can also deplete and the assumption is that addiction is associated with the diminution of capital and recovery with its growth.

- *Assertive linkage:* Although this has primarily been used in the past to link clients into AA groups, the philosophy is applied here to link in to other community resources including sports and recreation activities, education and training, peer activities and volunteering. Assertive linkage applies to supportive and engaging techniques to actively engage excluded populations with resources and assets in their communities.
- *Ongoing peer participation:* Based on the idea that generating a growing community of peer champions increases the viability and feasibility of recovery in the community and strengthens that community by its presence and its activities. Peers are seen as an essential part of a community coalition and as central to the process of engagement for people with addiction (and offending) histories.
- *Asset based community development:* The idea that communities have strengths and resources that are available and accessible to support recovery pathways and journeys, and that tapping into those resources is essential for bridging people through transitions to their own communities.

As with all of the projects included in the connections model, the aim is to bring together a number of key research and theoretical positions to develop a coherent approach to supporting and engaging vulnerable and excluded populations. The only one of these that has not really been discussed in any depth is the assertive linkage model and this will be outlined now. Following earlier work in the US by Timko and colleagues (2006), which had shown that people who had intensive referrals to mutual aid groups had better short- and long-term outcomes, I was involved in replicating this project in a UK context.

In a randomised trial led by Dr Victoria Manning, 153 consecutive admissions to an emergency ward at a south London psychiatric hospital were randomly assigned to three conditions. The first option was that they received a leaflet providing information about the mutual aid groups that were available around the hospital; in the second condition the doctor responsible for booking the patients in and conducting their initial assessment recommended that they attend at least one

AA, Narcotics Anonymous (NA) or Cocaine Anonymous (CA) meeting during their planned stay of 10 days. In the third condition, a peer from one of the groups came to talk to the patient about the group, offering to take them to a meeting and then to meet for a coffee to discuss how the meeting had gone afterwards.

While there was relatively poor uptake in the leaflet and doctor conditions, in the peer (assertive linkage) condition, there were three key findings. First, those patients attended more meetings on the ward as might be expected; second, they attended more 12-step meetings in the three months after discharge; and third, they reported lower levels of substance use in the three months after their discharge from the hospital. What is the point of this study? One conclusion is that people who engage with 12-step groups do better and so encouraging them to attend and supporting them to do so is important. However, there is a second implication that is every bit as important and that is that providing 'human bridges' to recovery supportive resources in the community is essential to improved client outcomes. It is also significant that this speaks to the key role of peers in acting as bridges for people attempting to reintegrate into the community.

To translate this into the language of recovery capital, excluded and marginalised groups like drinkers and drug users typically have limited access to pro-social groups and networks. Additionally, early in recovery people will often have low confidence and low self-esteem and so will be reluctant to push themselves forward for new groups and activities. Thus, assertive linkage both exposes people early in recovery to community capital and also provides them with the social support needed for them to actively engage with and benefit from such groups. While the groups involved in the trial were mutual aid 12-step groups, they do not have to be, and this process would work just as well with a football or a fishing club, or with volunteering schemes in the local community. And that is the model that underpinned the connections model in the Salvos centre in Dooralong. The aim would be to use the knowledge and networks of each connector to decide which groups they should connect to.

Procedure at Dooralong Recovery Centre

Participants

The initial set of participants were around 60 individuals connected to the Salvation Army. This consisted of current employees at the TC, former residents in the community (who had settled in the community since graduating) and other key Salvation Army staff who were potential community links, while several of the participants fulfilled more than one of these roles. Individuals were not asked to specify their status as part of a process of creating a coalition around community recovery rather than focusing on the individual status of participants. They were asked to undertake two tasks.

Task 1 involved splitting the overall group into five sub-groups based on the areas they lived or worked in to map out the community resources they were aware of and had previously engaged with. Groups were asked to identify three groups:

- individuals who could support active engagement in recovery groups and activities and social networks that would be free from the risk of drinking and drug use;
- informal groups and associations in the local community such as mutual aid groups, sports and recreation groups and other community groups; and
- institutions and organisations that could provide practical resources and supports.

The groups were asked to start the task and then complete it through emails and follow-up meetings. The key aims of this, learned from the Dandenong initiative, include building new relationships and establishing the connector group as a new asset. At the end of the initial session, as is typically the case for ABCD mapping, the sub-groups by location were asked to report back to the overall group and agree on next steps around engaging the community assets identified.

Task 2, undertaken in the same sub-groups, was based on geographic area, predicated on the idea that effective and sustainable community engagement must be based on mutual benefit and should be based on the idea that the TC – building, staff and residents – represents an opportunity to provide a valuable resource for the local community. This involves not only volunteering and working but actively engaging with a range of community groups. The reason for this is to challenge stigma through active participation and contribution to the local community. Within this task, there were two activities:

1. To consider methods for addressing what unmet needs in the local community could be addressed by the TC.
2. To identify resources and opportunities from within the TC to address these local community needs.

Findings and conclusions from the TC implementation process

We described these two tasks as 'reciprocal community development' and this is about being explicit that the residents had something important to offer to the community and that they were a valuable resource. This is a key message both for a marginalised group who may not see their own value but also to challenge assumptions in the community that this group should be seen either as a burden or as a case for special charity. Thus, the community development model is reciprocal.

The model is illustrated in Figure 2.2 and then explained; after which, the findings from the Dooralong project are outlined.

The figure depicts the complex interplay of professional organisations that the residents of the TC are linked to (on the left hand side of the figure). Residents have existing connections to health and welfare, criminal justice and substance use treatment systems that represent a form of helping capital and provide a potential bridge to a range of professional expertise and resource. This is not to assume that all of the residents will view professionals in this light or regard their contacts positively, but this remains an important area to explore and measure, and the commitment of many professionals (and their contributions to the community) should not be overlooked.

However, on the right hand side of the diagram is the more traditional territory of asset based approaches consisting of resources available in the community. In this project, there

Figure 2.2: Therapeutic landscape recovery among people with histories of substance use and offending

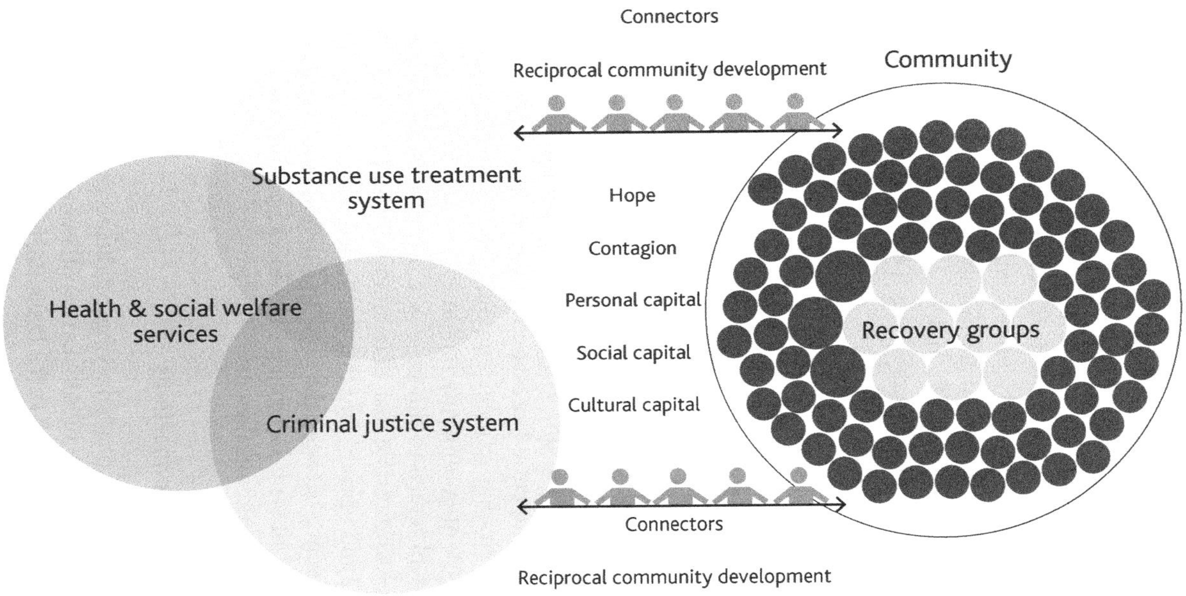

was a very specific goal of merging the assets in statutory and voluntary organisations with more local and informal groups and associations. Thus, the aim is to create a dynamic and strengths-based approach that links four groups into an active coalition:

- professionals and the agencies they represent;
- communities and groups, and people who can connect to various groups and are members of them;
- residents of the TC; and
- staff and volunteers at the TC, many of whom will be in long-term recovery.

The aim is to create social networks and associations between connectors across all four of these populations with a clear aspiration of building a network of links that are sustainable over time, and that build enduring strengths and community cohesion and wellbeing. To address the sustainability issue, the aim of this is to create a new group that is engaging and attractive and that will retain members and attract new members to the recovery coalition. This is entirely consistent with the notion of a therapeutic landscape for recovery, as the immediate goal of improving resident outcomes also contributes to a broader process of community building.

I will return to this issue in Chapter 4, but the key goal here is to demonstrate that all communities have strengths (including TCs and prisons) and that the bridges help not only to improve coherence between the two but also build social and community capital in each location – and do so by a process of contagion of hope and engagement.

Dooralong connections

The first task of identifying candidate community connectors yielded a total of 69 names of people who are linked to Dooralong through staff, clients and graduates and their personal connections in the Salvation Army, through the mutual aid groups and through their involvement in the local community. This group split into four to cover four distinct geographic areas and each outlined a number of recovery groups and local community resources such as Men's Shed, neighbourhood centres and youth centres, as well as Salvation Army groups such as the Women to Women Group, the Parenting Group and the Hope Group.

Key local groups and institutions identified in different sites included football (Australian Rules Football) and soccer clubs, further education colleges and universities, the Lions Club, drumming and dance clubs, Board riders, Community Fire Authority, neighbourhood centres and the local library. These are strong resources that constitute the right-hand side of Figure 2.2 and represent the traditional targets for connection. However, the initial workshop also had an additional component that was focused on creating the reciprocal component of the community engagement process. There will always be assets unique to communities and each connector group will have their own ideas about what the ideal starting point would be (and the preparations and support each person will need to help them engage effectively and integrate into new groups).

Reciprocating assets

In response to the question "What skills and assets do we have within our Dooralong community of staff and participants that could help to meet some of those needs?", three groups addressed what the TCs could contribute to the wellbeing of the local community, and there were general categories of support suggested (odd jobs, restoration and clean up, transport, volunteering) as well as utilisation of the physical resources owned by the Salvos (for instance, for functions and community activities, and to provide ongoing community hubs). There was not only the development of existing support to graduated residents but also the extension of this work to other vulnerable populations such as young mothers and substance users in the community. It was suggested that the greatest resources the TC could contribute to the local communities were in the form of people and time. There were specific skills and capabilities that could be tapped into in the form of drivers (with vehicles), landscaping and gardening, peer support, coordinating local volunteering options and skilled labour – often enhanced through tools and equipment owned by the Salvation Army.

The roll-out of the project involved the operationalisation of these activities, although we were not able to capture systematic data around implementation. This work continues and has led to increased utilisation of the facilities of the Dooralong Recovery Centre and increased two-way communication and engagement with a diverse range of local communities. However, it is a source of considerable frustration that we do not have adequate data on the impact this has had on the residents involved in the local community or on the wider community itself. This is in part the nature of such projects as the commitment to the activity should be stronger than the commitment to its evaluation but many of the exciting activities and processes remain relatively untested.

Conclusions and implications

In both of these initiatives a community connections model was successfully implemented in very diverse settings – one an urban setting involving a magistrates' court and the other a therapeutic community in a rural setting. Both communities had high levels of deprivation and poverty that did not prevent there being a diverse range of community assets that many professionals, peers and clients/residents were able to identify and to tap into through their existing knowledge and networks. Both settings also provided a significant opportunity for adding three core elements to the ABCD approach:

1. The first was an explicit partnership between professionals, clients and a diverse range of community stakeholders that created a coalition with multiple community stakeholders.
2. A model of 'reciprocal' community development where the underlying assumption, made explicit in the course of the project, is that the client group also constitutes a resource that has something valuable to contribute to overall community wellbeing.
3. The group itself becomes an emerging asset that can support growth and wellbeing in the community.

All of these objectives are central to the idea that the aim of these initiatives is twofold – to increase the likelihood of effective reintegration and long-term wellbeing for vulnerable and marginalised individuals and, through doing so, to generate community connections and strengths, and the overall wellbeing and connectedness of the communities the initiatives are carried out in. This is about challenging exclusionary and stigmatising attitudes among the general public to address some of the barriers of multiple exclusion that vulnerable populations experience, but also about building new networks and associations that can support long-term pathways to change. The latter goal is primarily about enriching communities by building new community assets, through empowering and connecting a group of champions drawn from all sections of the community.

So the aim of this work has a fundamental social justice component. The aim is to challenge exclusion and stigma and to create social binds as a consequence, and access to community resources that would otherwise be denied marginalised groups. The World Health Organization (2001) reported that drug addiction was the most stigmatised condition (and alcohol addiction the fourth most stigmatised) and the UK Drug Policy Commission (2010) reported on the extent and impact of stigma on wellbeing and capacity of individuals to re-engage through complex and insidious process of self-stigmatisation. Further, there is a perception that drug users are lacking in self-discipline and willpower (Jones et al, 2010); and that they are 'dirty' and disrespectful towards themselves and others (Sloan, 2012). Likewise, the public perceives people who offend as uneducated and unhygienic (Hirschfield and Piquero, 2010), deviant (MacLin and Herrera, 2006) and blameworthy (Lacey and Pickard, 2015). Overcoming these perceptions and generating real belief that people can change is a major challenge for all of those involved in supporting the process of recovery and rehabilitation.

Crucially, from the perspective of community connections, stigma goes beyond stereotyping and connotes a separation of 'us' from 'them' (Link and Phelan, 2001). The exclusion or othering of such populations has two effects – it decreases community coherence and integration, and it reduces the likelihood of effective reintegration for individuals who are marginalised and excluded. This is particularly important in the context of the community building component of this work as it is predicated on a social inclusion and a social justice approach, where effective reintegration relies on community capital and openness to marginalised populations re-engaging across a range of domains such as housing, education, employment and community groups.

For this to be achieved, there is a strong need for bridge building and developing meaningful pathways that assertively challenge exclusion and promote active reintegration. This is predicated on a core assumption of recovery-oriented models (White, 2009; Sheedy and Whitter, 2009): that recovery is a shared pathway that presumes an equality of status between the person in recovery and the peer navigators or clinicians they work with. So this model is replicated at a community level – there is an assumption of reciprocation in which it is assumed that not only do recovery communities have needs (social and community capital) but they also have resources that will enhance and enrich the communities they live in. As a consequence the outcome is a positive sum not a neutral state, with the twin goals of creating a therapeutic landscape and of improving the quality of life in the community for all of its members.

Key lessons

- Communities in even the most deprived and disadvantaged areas have assets and resources that can be mobilised to support recovery and reintegration, and each project identified a large number (and remarkable diversity) of assets in the communities involved.

- Mobilising such assets is a process that is generative and that can gather momentum and build hope – creating new assets and pathways to inclusion along the way.

- Assets alone are not sufficient and key individuals are needed to take on the role of community connectors to build and sustain the bridges, and to work with both vulnerable individuals and community groups to make the connections sustainable.

- This is a two-way street and it is assumed that the clients who are the target group for the project will also have assets that can be utilised to strengthen the community, and this is core to the idea of community growth.
- As a consequence, the aim is both to improve reintegration pathways and to build sustainable resources that strengthen local communities, making them more inclusive and better connected.
- Creating a therapeutic landscape for reintegration and recovery is intrinsically linked to an inclusive model of social justice.

Note

1 In this initiative, the project created a sustainable group of recovery connectors whose diverse backgrounds and experiences generated a vibrant and viable collaboration.

3

What do you need to recover? Jobs, Friends and Houses

Introduction and overview

This chapter will describe an innovative project – Jobs, Friends and Houses – that was developed in the north-west of England to help drug users and offenders reintegrate into their local communities. The aim was to inspire people to believe that their lives could change by engaging them in a programme that offered apprenticeships to employment linked to the renovation of poor quality housing. The housing would be transformed into recovery housing that they would be able to live in, forming a part of a recovery community. This model created a vibrant and visible social network of recovery that provided a pro-social network and access to a variety of meaningful activities and social supports. What the chapter will describe is the background and rationale for the project, its growth and development and my part in evidencing its impact and effectiveness. Towards the end of the chapter I will also describe an innovative method that I used with colleagues to test some of the key elements of social networks, based on the use of Facebook.

This work will build on the previous chapter in that it will focus on how belonging is critical in establishing a positive sense of hope and provides the foundations for effective engagement with resources in the community, and this chapter will initiate a discussion about how this links to ideas of identity, and in particular social identity. However, the basic rationale draws heavily on what the evidence base suggests are core foundations for recovery. The overall academic rationale for Jobs, Friends and Houses can be predicated on the three key things that have the strongest evidence base for working in recovery services – peer support, mutual aid and recovery housing (Humphreys and Lembke, 2013). It is no coincidence that all three of these have peer involvement and peer support as core components of their delivery.

What did Jobs, Friends and Houses set out to do and why?

In both the recovery and desistance literature there is a strong and consistent evidence base around meaningful activities. Laub and Sampson (2003) reported on a 55-year follow-up study of a cohort of juvenile offenders, one of the longest research studies in the social sciences, and concluded that the key predictors of desisting from offending could be summarised as 'informal social control', which consisted of attachment to pro-social support, primarily through acquiring a stable partner and remaining in suitable and rewarding employment. Sampson and Laub (2003: 46) argued that 'job stability, commitment to work and mutual ties binding workers and employers increase informal social control and, all else equal, lead to a cessation in criminal behaviour'. It is well evidenced from both the mental health (RETHINK, 2008) and from the addictions fields (Jason et al, 2007; Mericle et al, 2015) that recovery housing is an essential starting point in supporting recovery journeys. These core issues of employment and housing are combined in Jobs, Friends and Houses, the primary aim of which is outlined below.

Jobs, Friends and Houses (JFH) was a social enterprise supported by Lancashire Police and led by a sergeant from the police force, Steve Hodgkins, to provide employment opportunities in the construction industry for people in recovery from alcohol and drug addiction, with a particular focus on those coming out of local prisons, supported by a programme manager who is in long-term recovery and who is well connected in the recovery and business communities in Blackpool. It targets those seeking to sustain recovery from addiction, by assisting them to build a sustainable future consisting of recovery support, pathways to recovery housing and a route to employment regardless of their previous employment and offending history. JFH has a specific stream that targets individuals newly released from prison, although referrals are also taken from a range of community sources, and this has grown as the reputation of the organisation has expanded. The primary aim of JFH is to create a successful business (primarily construction related) that will employ people in recovery and contribute towards the development of recovery housing in Blackpool. However, what JFH provides is a sense of hope and purpose but also a highly visible and positive social identity for people aspiring to long-term recovery and reintegration.

The basic model of JFH as a social enterprise was to buy houses or business premises, renovate or refurbish them and either sell them for profit that will be re-invested in the business or rent them out as recovery housing, although the funding model evolved and JFH increasingly engaged in a partnership with a property developer. To achieve this, they engaged a workforce that consists of a combination of trained professionals (joiners, plumber, electrician, plasterer, bricklayer, project manager) who mentored and trained up programme trainees, with some of the tradesmen having lived experience and others no prior contact to working with people with addiction histories. These programme participants start as volunteers and, if suitable, are enrolled on an initial eight-week building course with the local further education college (Blackpool and Fylde College). If successful in this phase, participants work on JFH building projects while undertaking an apprenticeship in an appropriate building qualification, depending on the needs of JFH and the aptitudes and interests they have developed. They were also effectively building housing that they could aspire to live in and that would become a part of the recovery community in Blackpool.

As both Best and colleagues (2008) in the UK and Longabaugh and colleagues (2010) in the US have shown, the key to successfully sustaining a recovery journey is to bring about the transition from a social network that is supportive of substance use to one that is supportive of recovery. What JFH has achieved is to provide a strong and inclusive social network and then to supplement that with effective linkage to a range of recovery and other pro-social activities (see the section on community asset mapping later in this chapter, where this effect is shown in more detail). However, there is an additional element to this belonging that is crucially important, which is around visible identity. In contrast to the anonymous mutual aid fellowships, JFH created a very high profile identity in which the logo of the organisation was clearly depicted on the work outfits of the participants (and all the other staff), on the vans and cars they were transported in and in signs on all of the buildings that JFH worked on.

This created a strong (and positive) brand that would be recognised as professional and central to the regeneration of the town, and so generate a social identity that JFH participants could be proud to be a part of. This notion of identity is crucial to the first part of our research investigations where my colleagues and I used a unique approach to assess identity, belonging and their effects on engagement with recovery supports. JFH also aimed to produce housing to the highest standards so that the residents, as well as the builders, could develop a sense of pride and self-respect based on being connected to JFH.

Using social media to measure social identity and social connections

In collaboration with colleagues from the University of Western Sydney and Monash University, I used a new set of data analysis measures to make the most of the open Facebook page that JFH created for their participants (Bliuc et al, 2017) to further our understanding of how this sense of belonging and positive identity emerges.

JFH set out not only to provide safe housing and meaningful occupations to its participants, but also to generate a sense of holistic wellbeing. This was achieved by encouraging new participants to join the local recovery community (and attend 12-step groups), but also by having a diverse range of social activities including photography, barbecues and visits to various local groups and activities. The rhetoric of JFH participants was around feeling that they were a part of a 'family' who worked together, recovered together and socialised together. This was supplemented by creating a Facebook page that provided a forum to tell people about JFH and also to provide a social support system online for participants in the programme. There is an intriguing evidence base emerging around social media, for example, recent research by Hobbs et al (2016) based on a large US dataset (12 million social media profiles) suggests that people who are well integrated in online social networks such as Facebook are likely to have lower mortality rates. Access to social support facilitated through online communication is particularly useful in cases of social, geographical or mobility-related isolation (Rodham et al, 2009; Savic et al, 2013). In this case, while the primary aim was around communicating with the outside world (to boost bridging capital) it played a very strong part in providing support and connection to those active in JFH (bonding capital).

Not only have online networks been used for providing standalone counselling and support, but they are also used as a supplement to face to face services. This was the result with JFH where the online group was evolving into a forum to provide additional support but also afforded a platform for the staff and participants in JFH to engage with a range of outside groups. Therefore, in the language of Putnam's (2000) model of social capital, it provided both bonding capital (increasing the strength of links between members of a group) and bridging capital (improving the connections between JFH participants and other groups and individuals). Through the latter strategy, it was part of an approach to increase community connections between JFH and outside groups for shared and mutual benefits, and provided a way to communicate and support members and the group as a whole.

From a research point of view, online activity offers a different kind of option and opportunity. There is a growing awareness that 'traditional scientific methods need to be expanded to deal with complex issues that arise as social systems meet technological innovation' (Shneiderman, 2008: 1349). An open Facebook page like the one that JFH had developed offers a real-time opportunity to look at changes in social networks and social group membership. The method for our study was that we made use of these affordances by using social network and textual data extracted from the group's Facebook page that is complemented by qualitative data from in-depth interviews with key agents in the network, and quantitative retention data. I had a strong bond with the JFH team, including the apprentices, and they were happy to trust me to use these data and to talk about what the Facebook page meant to them.

As a first measure of online engagement in the community of support, we looked at the growth in the online activity as captured by the number of posts and comments on the Facebook page, from the initial inception of the page, having obtained the appropriate ethical clearance, and discussed the project with both the staff and the participants in JFH. Our analysis was based on the idea of examining the online community of support as made up of three primary groups of members and the interactions between them: JFH programme participants; JFH staff; and external individuals (broader community members). The method of extracting online data is called 'scraping' and basically turns the posts on a Facebook page into text that can be stored on a standard Excel file. We then undertook two types of data analysis using different computer software packages – one to do Social Network Analysis and the other using linguistic software to make sense of the content of posts, based on a model called Linguistic Inquiry and Word Count (LIWC).

Social network analysis (SNA) is a comprehensive approach to understanding the relational features in groups (contacts, ties, connections, group attachments and encounters that relate one group member to another) so it provides an ideal tool to capture group dynamics (and the types of links to other groups) and communication in the JFH online community (Scott, 2012). The second analysis technique is linguistic analysis, which focused on linguistic markers of social identity and social group belonging in the current context. Changes in the social identity of group members are captured through conducting a computerised analysis of the language used by participants in their contributions to the Facebook page. By using LIWC we can identify the levels (and changes in these) of identification with the recovery group (Pennebaker, 2011), and the underlying emotions (Chung and Pennebaker, 2014; Gill et al, 2008). One of the interesting features of Facebook posts from a research point of view is that the 'likes' a post attracts constitute a form of reinforcement and endorsement from the group and so can be regarded as acceptance and a marker of group belonging.

We used programme retention as our measure of duration of staying in the recovery programme because this has previously been found to be associated to long-term positive recovery outcomes (Zhang et al, 2003). In other words, we looked for any relationship between what kind of interactions JFH clients had online and what their likelihood of staying in the programme was, given that we know that longer retention is associated with better outcomes.

Better social connections and more positive communications makes JFH participants stay in the programme for longer

In total, there were 609 participants in the online JFH Facebook community and this includes JFH programme participants (N = 23), JFH staff (N = 5), and other community members (N = 581) who contributed to the online discussions over a period of eight months following the establishment of the JFH Facebook page. In our analysis, we accessed all of the posts and likes on the Facebook page over the first eight months that it was operational and this was the basis for our analysis.

We found that programme retention is significantly determined by SNA centrality (which means that the more central people are in the online network, the longer they stay in the program). The second key finding was that, based on the linguistic inquiry method, we found that retention in the group was not only significantly predicted by the pronoun 'we' use (a social identity marker – the more they talk about 'we' the longer they stayed in the program), but also by the extent of affirmation or in-group validation – reflected in the number of comments and post 'likes' received (that is, other people liked their post), comment 'likes' received, and all 'likes' received.

It is important to note that while collective personal pronoun use ('we') is predictive of retention, individual personal pronoun ('I') was not. What this implies is that the salience of the group (and the individual's commitment and belonging to it) are associated with greater endorsement by the group and longer engagement in it. So this would appear to be a dynamic process in which an increased sense of commitment and belonging are associated with greater support from and endorsement by other members of the group. Perceiving yourself as a member of a group means others are more likely to support and endorse what you say which in turn links to how central you are to the virtual social network in the group.

There was one other aspect of the study that helped us validate the findings from the analysis of the Facebook posts. We managed to track down two individuals who progressed from the periphery of the group to the centre, and asked them to complete in-depth interviews about their experiences. Both of the people we interviewed were male, and they were aged 30 and 45. Participant 1 started with JFH in mid-January 2015, and in his own words, before joining the community, he was addicted and homeless, living in a shelter. Participant 2 joined JFH from the start of the community (01/11/2014), and before that he was "on the sick [Disability Living Allowance] and working part-time – abstinent about one year – living in a recovery house – not a lot of support in the house – working in services taking clients on prescriptions to the gym, 16 hours a week".

They were able to corroborate the twin benefits of online support group participation and the impact it had had for them.

The interviewees valued the availability of online communication with other group members ('live social connectivity') and they saw it as an asset that supports their recovery. One of them said: "It's good, sometimes you get notifications like 'has anyone seen T?' – and you get five phone calls. It is a really good support network … it's visible … it reminds me that you are part of something." This is the bonding capital component of the social network in that it helps to strengthen the bonds between members of the group. However, there is also a bridging component.

The same interviewee went on to say:

> 'what excites me more is when other people comment. It just gives me a really good feeling. … It shows the support from the people who are out there. … It's like the ripple effect – instead of parents

> writing off their children, they are starting to have some sense of hope.'

This is critical in understanding the importance of community engagement for an excluded and marginalised group – they come to see themselves differently as a consequence of their active engagement with the wider community. This was also a theme that emerged in the other interview with the participant stating that, "It's like the wider community coming in. … It's about the recovery community getting in touch with the wider community – and it's important that it is about the wider community and them understanding – like that incident with the woman" (reference to an incident when several members of the groups intervened and saved a woman in a domestic incident, written up in Best, 2016).

The concluding comment from the first interviewee shows how important the members of the group saw their networking on social media to be.

> 'You will go out your way if you need to bring other people on board … a lot of guys, it has given them hope. A lot of people are touched through addiction, and now they can see that there is hope. They are looking at them differently and they can see that there is hope. … Really important (to be seen as successful); we are visible – we can recover and we can deal with everyday stuff – without individuals to show that it does work, it wouldn't seem the same … Where you are now and where you were two years ago…'

In many ways this interview epitomises the important aspects of how a recovery community engages with the wider community and the central role that the social transmission of hope plays in this process. There is a very clear sense, which participants in the JFH programme were aware of, that they acted as ambassadors for recovery and that they had an important role in both challenging stigma and in actively engaging with the community for mutual benefit. There is a dynamic relationship between pride and identity within the group and the confidence and capacity to engage effectively with other groups.

The analysis of the JFH Facebook group showed that the salience of the group and the individuals' commitment and belonging are associated with greater endorsement by the group and longer engagement in it. Our findings in this study support the argument that developing a sense of collective selfhood (a positive recovery identity) helps the recovery process, but that for this to be sustainable it has to be embedded in prosocial bonds. However, the second part of the analysis of JFH will look at the links to the community and how they influenced the recovery pathways of participants.

Community connections and outcomes at JFH

The analysis that I led into JFH was a one-year evaluation that included an outcomes component. Overall, this showed clear improvements in three areas – offending, substance use and wellbeing, and these outcomes were clearly associated with spending longer in the programme, and this is linked to a strong sense of connection.

The average social network size of JFH participants rose from 32 to 98 on average with a strong recovery and broader community network. This was also linked to a very strong emerging social identity around recovery and around JFH as twin pillars of a positive identity that allowed those involved with JFH to have a sense of pride, dignity and purpose. In the qualitative interviews, this was strongly associated, both in the minds of the JFH staff and outside key informants, as a visible community of hope that was strongly bound together through their joint activities and the successes of the business enterprise.

In the evaluation, the extent of change in key offending domains was incredible. Before joining JFH, the 48 clients who were involved in the first year evaluation work had a total of 1142 recorded offences on the Police National Computer (an average of 32 per person), over criminal careers lasting 13 years, suggesting extremely high and change-resistant criminal involvement. Twenty-eight JFH staff had experienced a total of 176 imprisonments before the start of JFH. Since joining JFH, a total of five offences had been recorded (by three individuals). This means that the average annual offence rate was 2.46 before they joined JFH and 0.15 since joining JFH. This represents a 94.1% reduction in the annual recorded offence rate, which is an incredible success rate massively exceeding what would normally be expected from rehabilitation programmes.

The strength of JFH lay in part in a series of networks that pre-dated JFH through the police, the recovery and mutual aid communities, through the specialist addiction treatment services, and into the business and arts communities. While these have evolved and grown over time, the leadership of JFH had strong social capital they could link in to and these networks have coalesced as JFH has developed a strong business and community reputation, ensuring that it is seen as a key part of the Blackpool community. At least a part of the process of such dramatic improvement in offending was around the effective integration of these groups into pro-social communities, in which wellbeing support and business engagement were added to the traditional pillars of recreation, work and education, community engagement and mutual aid.

Thus, while it is clear that JFH participants benefited from a sense of hope provided by the core components of a safe place to live in recovery housing and a meaningful role during their apprenticeship, there was also a crucial component of the project that was about community connectedness, with all of the key links to recreational activities, mutual aid and the community and employment and training. However, JFH also had a different set of links through the business and housing groups in the town that were beneficial to the running of a business but also as a means of building bridges to new groups in the community both at a collective and an individual level. In the original ABCD model, McKnight and Block (2010: 132) have argued that building integrated and supportive communities rests on 'more individual connections and more associational connections', which in turn relies on identifying those who have the capacity to connect others in our communities. Community asset mapping was a core component of the evaluation of JFH and one of the primary aims was around creating sustainable pathways for full community reintegration.

It is also important to note that assets are specific to the context in which they are studied and accounted for. Thus, while the basic set of assets linked to sports and recreation, employment and training, mutual aid and community volunteering provide a starting point, it is critical to understand that each area will have its own unique strengths and its particular configuration of groups that flourish and promote community wellbeing, and the same is true for connectors. The idea of the model is not to tap into every single asset in an area, but to build connections to assets that fit and where there are links that can be established and built upon.

It is evident from this that the unique impact of JFH was across a series of domains where some of the contacts had resulted from the earlier individual and personal networks of key JFH stakeholders. There were a series of tentative connections in the area of sport and recreation and emerging business partnerships. JFH was in the process of converting these from personalised relationships to 'corporate' connections in which the whole organisation was linked to enable continuity of contact and strong pathways represented by a range of community connectors. In doing so, JFH embodied one of the core objectives of the asset model which is to translate personalised connections (that have the risk of disappearing when the individuals leave or the friendship is severed) to more sustainable pathways between groups and organisations. While every team and group will have local links, these cannot be exclusively reliant on a small number of personal relationships and one of the central aims of a connectors model is to build sustainability and evolution in the relationships that exist. Furthermore, what served JFH well was that each of the domains of connection provided access into a new local set of resources that could contribute to the recovery and rehabilitation of the project participants in different ways.

The evolution and development of assets

This sense of evolution and growth is evidenced in the follow-up data collected at one year after the establishment of JFH, which does not indicate a growth in the number of organisations that JFH was connected to but does show an increase in the strength of the bind (linking capital) and the ability to be a key partner in the various communities (which could be referred to as bonding and bridging capital combined). Thus, for JFH, building up of the links into the business community was a critical component of establishing the organisation as well as of building links at personal, commercial and community levels. The effect of this transition is that the connection becomes less reliant on individuals and in the pathways model outlined here, the path is more robust and durable between the clients of JFH and the wider community. In education and training this included both charities and local organisations, as well as colleges and universities, employers who offered initial volunteering opportunities and vocational support groups.

It became evident that there are a large number of organisations who have some connections to each other but JFH has positioned itself through a commitment to network development so that it has evolved into being a central player in this arena. This not only increases the options for JFH participants to access different types of community resources, but it also increases the reach of JFH into organisations that can provide potential connectors and supporters to their core work.

For JFH, these maps were developed across multiple domains and became indicative of how effectively JFH had become a part of multiple communities and groups in Blackpool. They were able to provide increasing diversity to participants in the programme to meet their needs and the stage of their recovery journey and this includes strong connections to the Blackpool Recovery Group, Families In Recovery, SMART Recovery and a number of 12-step mutual aid groups. However, it also included local recovery activities and groups, including a Saturday Night Social Club, and a group for people in recovery and their partners.

This is probably the most significant asset map in terms of the development of the networks that are needed to support early recovery but may become less important as participants develop a more diverse and personal recovery network. Thus, there are options there for people whose aim is not abstinence, there are recovery-focused social activities (such as the Sunday night social club) and there is a Family Recovery Group to support those with children. These are markers suggesting the emergence of a therapeutic landscape of recovery, where recovery groups are linked and support each other, and the participant has support and opportunity to engage with a variety of recovery groups depending on their own belief systems as well as their stage of recovery. This means that JFH staff and project participants can fill their days with activities early in their recovery journey and then gradually become more selective as their social supports change and they start to identify groups and activities commensurate with their interests, talents and passions.

Over the course of the first year of JFH, there were two primary changes:

1. The locus of connection was more likely to be the organisation than simply one member, suggesting increases in sustainability.
2. The bonds became stronger and were more likely to be on an equal footing with JFH in the role of giving back to the community and participating in its activities.

The latter point is critical to the idea of reciprocal community development outlined in the previous chapter as what this suggests is that JFH became established as a core part of the system both providing and accessing support as needed. This is central to the idea that the overall aim is a positive sum and the generation of new assets at a community level. Overall, there is a clear indication of important embeddedness for JFH and a strengthening of both bonding and linking capital, and much clearer indications of the contribution that JFH is making to life in Blackpool. JFH clients are not afforded special treatment in groups and activities and are expected to be positive contributors, as would be expected within a reciprocal community development model.

Conclusions and some thoughts about social identity

JFH has become rapidly established as a core component of the recovery community in Blackpool and is clearly seen as a beacon of hope, not only by staff and participants in the project but also by the broader community where JFH has had an active role not only in rehabilitation but also in community regeneration through the work done around the renovation of run-down housing, replacing it with highly desirable properties and a sense of community participation and active engagement. JFH has worked with a highly marginalised and excluded population and has given them a sense of pride and belonging and the support systems to nurture their own personal journeys to recovery.

The impact on the client group is evident with the reported improvements in offending and substance use, and clear improvements in wellbeing and quality of life for those involved, over the course of the first year of the programme. However, there is also a broader impact that is shown in the social media analysis where JFH creates not only strong internal bonds but strong links to a wide range of other community groups. It is here that the issue of identity arises, which has significant ramifications for people from excluded and marginalised groups who are attempting to reintegrate. This final section of this chapter will discuss the issue of social identity and recovery, and what was unique about the JFH approach to this.

For many years, identity change has been regarded as a critical part of the process of both desistance from offending and recovery from substance use. Biernacki (1986) argued that, in order to achieve recovery, 'addicts must fashion new identities, perspectives and social world involvements wherein the addict identity is excluded or dramatically depreciated' (Biernacki, 1986: 141). Building on this theme, McIntosh and McKeganey (2000, 2002) collected the recovery narratives of 70 former addicts in Glasgow, Scotland, and concluded that, through substance misuse, the addicts' 'identities have been seriously damaged by their addiction' (McIntosh and McKeganey, 2002: 152). On this basis, they argued that recovery required the restoration of a currently 'spoiled' identity. This model has been critiqued by Neale et al (2011), who have contended that the notion of a spoiled identity is pejorative and that it neglects the range of alternative identities available to individuals across different social contexts (such as father, daughter, neighbour, and so on) and overemphasises the salience and primacy of the identity associated with substance misuse. Each person has multiple identities – father, neighbour, woman, Scottish, Minecraft expert player – but what is important is the salience of each of these identities and how widely they influence the person's attitudes and behaviour.

However, this is all predicated on the idea that identity is primarily personal and more recent theories have come to focus on the impact on identity of social group membership. The social identity model of recovery (SIMOR; Best et al, 2016) frames recovery as a process of social identity change in which a person's most salient identity shifts from being defined by membership of a group whose norms and values revolve around substance abuse to being defined by membership of a group whose norms and values encourage recovery. For this model to apply, the new group that the person aspires to join has to be attractive and have characteristics that will diminish the exclusion and stigma that their previous lifestyle has encompassed. Social identities are embedded in personal, social and cultural capital and so it is not easy to ask people to change their social networks or their social identities.

What is intriguing about JFH from a social identity perspective is that the organisation has promoted a very visible form of positive identity through the company logo being emblazoned on all of the vans and on the sides of the buildings that they were working on. But much more importantly, all of the high visibility jackets, polo shirts and hats were also marked with the JFH logo. In other words, far from being anonymous, JFH set out to create a visible and recognisable identity that would be associated with recovery and community engagement in Blackpool. Thus, the success of JFH as a community connections project was not only about active engagement with and participation in the local community but also creating a model of recovery community that challenged exclusion stereotypes and beliefs. This was part of an ethos of trying to develop properties to a very high standard to ensure that they generated pride among the workforce and a positive reputation in the wider community.

JFH created a model of hope that was contagious but contagious not only for those in recovery but for a whole community, which increasingly came to engage with what was seen as a massive success and a source of inspiration. That this is no longer operating in the same way in Blackpool is not a reflection on the model or those who championed it but on a group of officials and professionals who were not able to let it flourish. However, that is another story and there are signs that JFH will be back in a stronger and more visible form soon. JFH generated a huge amount of local interest based on the fact that the benefits were experienced significantly beyond the recovery community and, in spite of subsequent challenges relating to governance and organisational factors, remains a key exemplar of innovation and community engagement.

Key lessons

- Engaging in positive recovery communities is an active process that involves a sense of commitment and belonging to the group and to the values it holds.
- Although there are many pathways to recovery, JFH is a strong example of visible recovery as a means of actively engaging the community and challenging stigma and exclusion through combining the mobilisation of assets and active engagement in a range of meaningful activities.
- Using a new technique of data scraping, combined with Social Network Analysis and linguistic word count analysis, we were able to show that being central to the group, a sense of belonging and being actively endorsed by other group members predicted better recovery outcomes.
- JFH was highly successful in addressing offending and substance use and did so by providing hope and meaning – and by providing connections to pro-social groups, both through the work offered and in additional group activities.
- One of the keys to the JFH success was its capacity to provide a complex and growing network of community connections.

- What the evaluation of JFH showed was that it is possible for those links to grow over time and to strengthen through regular use by multiple individuals within the group.
- Part of this growth was increasing embeddedness in a range of community networks with JFH providing a great example of reciprocal community development.
- JFH helped to foster recovery identities by providing a strong and positive social identity that created the opportunity for individuals to find their own paths to recovery.

4

Keep it in the family: the role of families in supporting the rehabilitation of prisoners

The following chapter is based on work conducted primarily at HMP Kirkham, which is an adult male Category D open prison in the north-west of England (near Preston), holding over 650 prisoners. Category D prisons are largely for prisoners in the last two years of long sentences and are designed to support reintegration back into the community.

The prison has a focus on rehabilitation and reintegration upon release, with numerous programmes and initiatives being developed within the prison, including the 'Bridge to Change' programme developed by the governor to prepare prisoners for release. The basic aim of this project is to prepare long-sentence prisoners for reintegration back into the community, with prisoners transferring to Kirkham when they have around two years left of their sentences to serve. This fits within the broader rehabilitative culture that UK prisons have focused on to support effective reintegrative work as a core part of prison culture.

This chapter will outline the evidence around prisoner reintegration back into the community and the risks of reoffending before the introduction of the innovative programme based on community connections trialled there, and the implications the programme has for the development of the reciprocal community connections model.

Background and evidence around prison release and reoffending

Upon release from prison in the UK, 44% of adults will be reconvicted within one year, costing the economy up to £13 billion per annum (National Audit Office, 2010), in addition to the huge emotional and personal toll not only on prisoners but also on their families and communities. The need for interventions that support the successful re-entry and reintegration of released prisoners is demonstrated by rates of recidivism and overcrowding (Hunter et al, 2016); for ex-prisoners who are also experiencing recovery from addiction, re-entry is potentially twice as difficult, with issues of both withdrawal and stigma potentially compounding the challenges. Additional issues including housing and mental health and other possible problems around reintegration, and the willingness of both professionals and communities to support attempts at reintegration. Bonds can be destabilised by changing living arrangements as well as changes, values and behaviours, particularly with familial relationships, where the gaps caused by the time spent in prison has the ability to reduce trust and weaken social bonds (Wolff and Draine, 2004).

Therefore, to bridge the gap between prison and the community, relationships and their resources must be consistently supported and mobilised by resettlement programmes to facilitate the growth of a radius of trust (Fukuyama, 2001). Individuals who come out of prison will have all kinds of adjustments to make in leaving behind one peer group, and potentially attempting to avoid old peers associated with substance use and offending. All the while, they will be adjusting to the changes in their existing family relationships and adjusting to things that have changed during their period inside. In prison, visits from family or friends provides the opportunity to establish and enhance social support networks and can assist the formation of a pro-social identity (Duwe and Clark, 2012). In a study of male British prisoners, family relationships were shown to predict positive outcomes around accommodation, alcohol and drug use, coping with resettlement challenges and the quality of post-release family relations (Markson et al, 2015).

There is a cautionary note to this effect. In analysing the Serious and Violent Offenders Reentry Initiative, Boman and Mowen (2017) reported that while families can exert a strong protective effect during the re-entry phase, this is weaker than the risks associated with re-engaging with criminal peers. The authors concluded that while both families and peers exerted important effects, 'results also demonstrate that criminal peers significantly weaken the link between family support and the prevention of criminal recidivism' (Boman and Mowen, 2017: 767). Thus, family stability is important but it cannot be assumed that it is the only or even the primary social influence. Within a contagion model, social pressures can drive towards negative peer influence as well as positive group or family influence and this is a constant and ongoing journey between countervailing forces.

Nonetheless, in the UK, the Farmer Review (Farmer, 2017) has argued that not only does enhanced contact with families reduce reoffending rates, increased family contact may also help to break inter-generational transmission of offending and imprisonment, and the report has called for an increased focus on improving family involvement with prisoners and for innovations to support this process. In a similar vein, Hunter et al (2016) recommended that prisoner re-entry programmes: a) move away from risk-oriented approaches towards strengths-based support; b) coordinate with family and community resources and should facilitate the rebuilding of positive family relationships; and c) should build flexible and responsive, innovative programmes.

There are important philosophical changes in this transition, particularly the move towards a relational approach to rehabilitation, and the further acknowledgement of the benefits of strengths-based models. Rather than viewing individuals through a risk-oriented lens, which in itself can create barriers to overcoming challenges, strengths-based approaches focus on identifying skills and mobilising assets, based on principles of resilience, transformation, empowerment and civic engagement (Saleeby, 1996). This can create challenges for prison staff and governors who are generally trained to focus on risk minimisation and the importance of public protection in their duties.

The focus on families also adds an important temporal component in that it necessitates a future-oriented frame where family relationships inside prison are seen as supporting the wellbeing of prisoners while they are serving their sentences but also in supporting them to prepare for life once they return to the community. In this respect, the approach outlined below has both a future-oriented frame but one that is built on relational components of reintegration and provides the basis for a 'reintegration capital' where, as in the previous chapter, both immediate relationships and the relationship with more diverse aspects of the community is seen as central to supporting and enabling long-term change. In other words, building family relationships gives those in prison a form of social capital that should provide hope but also a clear motivation to avoid current and future substance use and offending.

The rationale and background to the Kirkham Family Connectors programme

In HMP Kirkham, as in most adult prisons, visits from friends and family members play an important role in the schedules of the prison, but one that carries security risks around the importation of drugs and other contraband such as mobile phones and weapons. This is every bit as much of a risk in open prisons as in more secure parts of the prison estate, and more so because there are no physical barriers between prisoners and their guests in the large open visiting hall at HMP Kirkham.

The rationale for the project was to supplement visiting time with a structured training programme for family members and prisoners to support pathways to effective reintegration into the community by reconciling two processes:

1. Identifying and mobilising appropriate community assets.
2. At the individual prisoner level, agreeing on interests and passions that the prisoner would like to pursue on their release from prison.

However, the project had the following underlying philosophical components:

- a strengths-based approach;
- embedded in a rehabilitative culture in the prison;
- a relational component based on all of the key participants – prisoners, family members and prison staff;
- an inclusive and participative model; and
- a focus on the wellbeing of all of the participants and stakeholders.

The basic rationale was similar to that outlined in Chapter 6, which focuses on community connectors in Sheffield, but what will be described here is the evolving rationale for community connections before overviewing the procedure and describing the results from the initial phases of application with families and prisoners.

The application of community connectors in a prison setting

While much of the focus of the previous chapters has been on recovery from substance use, the current chapter is more explicitly about the process of desistance from offending. The literature around desistance, while recognising that this is a process over time, has examined in more depth whether desistance is primarily driven by individual decisions and choices (motivation being a prime example) or about systems and structures (like marriage and jobs). Desistance research has also highlighted the critical role of familial bonds for reducing reoffending (Sampson and Laub, 2003; Laub et al, 1998).

Family attachments during a prison sentence can be crucial for managing the pressures of prison life, providing hope for when the prisoner is released, and in offering essential support during the resettlement process in the period immediately after release from prison (Naser and La Vigne, 2006; Rocque et al, 2013). As Brunton-Smith and McCarthy (2017) have argued, identifying opportunities for strengthening opportunities for family bonding and shared activities may be important in terms of building resources and relationships that will improve outcomes when individuals are released from prison.

In the current context, this has two significant conceptual foundations – first the building of a sense of hope, and second the generation of social capital that is linked to community engagement. In essence, the rationale for the prison based project is based on the idea that family members can act as human carriers of hope and undertake a relational role that links activities in prisons on the one hand with vibrant and socially inclusive communities on the other. This would be consistent with the suggestion from Rocque and colleagues (2013) that family visits improve the strength of familial attachment, which in turn reduces the propensity of prisoners to reoffend. Thus, the strength of bonds acts as a way of developing informal social control, which in turn increases commitment to pro-social behaviour.

It is easy to frame this in the language of both social capital and social identity theory. The fundamental aim of the project – and the underlying model – is about social contagion of hope building social connections and social capital resulting in improved wellbeing and a growing sense of belonging and empowerment. Watching this come to life in the Family Connectors project as it was rolled out was one of the most satisfying and rewarding experiences of my career.

It is important to reiterate the point from mental health about CHIME. In Leamy et al's (2011) review of what works in mental health recovery projects, successful interventions were generally considered to work on the basis of their capacity to promote and build Connectedness, Hope, Identity, Meaning and Empowerment. My own experiences would suggest that exactly the same is true for addiction recovery but the current capital model may offer us a clue of how this works. Putnam's model of social capital (2000) is predicated on the idea that the experience of accumulating resources is a combination of the strength of bonds within the groups we belong to (bonding capital) and the associations between the groups we belong to and other groups (bridging capital). However, in the OECD (2007) version they also talk about linking capital to connections to groups further up or down the social ladder. I will not discuss social ladders but the links to new groups that already have access to community resources is critical to this approach.

This is critically important in the current model of reintegration where the linkage component of social capital is about accessing groups that would otherwise have been considered beyond the reach of our populations of offenders and substance users, through processes of exclusion and stigmatisation compounded by their own internalisation of those negative and excluding stereotypes and perceptions about themselves (called self-stigma). Linkages to pro-social and valued groups in communities provide access to resources (human capital such as skills and education; cultural capital in terms of access to sporting and recreational activities and natural and built capital, which in turn means access to open and green spaces and to amenities within the community). However, as became apparent in the course of the project, it was not only the prisoners who benefited from these new connections but the family members as well.

Through this process, the excluded and vulnerable individuals are not only afforded opportunities to access resources, they also have the opportunity to re-calibrate their sense of empowerment, efficacy and confidence. Thus, personal capital can potentially grow as a consequence of this process through identifying strengths and using these to plan for the future. Further, this links to the concept of identity as accessing and engaging with positive and valued groups leads to a different kind of internalisation – which is the values, norms and beliefs of the positively valued groups (Jetten et al, 2012a; Haslam et al, 2012). As people engage in pro-social groups – including but not restricted to addiction recovery groups like 12-step fellowships – they internalise the processes that adhere in these groups and change as a result.

In summarising what we know about the psychological processes of change that take place in addiction recovery, Moos (2007) has argued that one of the effective elements of mutual aid groups like AA is the availability of opportunities for social learning provided by the observation of group members who are further into their recovery journeys. Moos goes further to argue that it is not just role models that AA offers but also an implicit expectation that new members will learn and conform to the group's norms to achieve and maintain membership, a process he refers to as 'social control'. This is entirely consistent with the informal social control model that has been advanced by Laub and Sampson (2003) in which the process of embedding in groups leads to a change of values. This can also be framed in the language of social identity.

As SIMOR (Best et al, 2016) has also posited, the process of supporting and facilitating individuals to move away from their using and offending groups and into pro-social groups and activities is not a straightforward process because of the ongoing pull of the using or offending groups, as well as the challenges linked to stigma and social exclusion, some of which will have been internalised, leaving the prisoners with low self-esteem and low self-efficacy. Thus, the process involved in the Kirkham Family Connectors project is around assertive linkage into positive groups – where inequalities at a community level are dealt with through processes of community mapping and assertive linkage.

In Kirkham, the rationale was to recruit a group of people in the period immediately prior to their release from prison, and to find viable and attractive pathways to pro-social groups that were linked to both their needs and their interests, but crucially also to what they saw as their passions and their strengths. What is unique about this project is that we attempted to use family members to make this connection. Described in the next section are the first two waves of Kirkham Family Connectors, who were recruited and trained to support the transition from prison to the community. The aim was to build up positive social capital for those leaving prison but in doing so also to create stronger connections from the prison to the community and to enhance social inclusion and community wellbeing in the wider community.

An evolving process

The first two iterations of the community connectors work are described separately as there was sufficient change in the programme between the first and second iteration that it does not make sense to combine them. This should provide the reader with a sense of how the programme changed in response to the feedback.

It is important to acknowledge the critical role that the staff played – and five staff members in particular. First, the then governor, Graham Beck, and his deputy, Dan Cooper (now the governor), provided unflinching support for the project from the start and ensured that any organisational barrier were surmounted successfully. Second, the Senior Probation Officer, Clare Ogden-Webb, and the two probation officers, Jacqui Dixon and Rob Heslop, become genuine champions for the project. At this point, it is worth noting that the core relational component of the initiative is reflected in the planning and implementation stages – the pleasure of working on the project, and the rapid contagion of its impact derive in large part from the energy and commitment of a range of key stakeholders and the emerging relationships that support this work.

In terms of an agreed objective for the project, the overall aim was to engage the help of prisoners' family and friends to aid this transition through their assertive linkage of the prisoner to productive and meaningful activities pre-release through three workshops across four weeks, by training them to become community connectors. At the request of the prisoners, we subsequently added a booster session to the programme around three months after the third session. It was anticipated that this would support the growth of hope for a positive future for both parties and create links that would enhance the likelihood of effective community reintegration on release.

In the initial iteration, following meetings with prison staff, the overall training design was agreed to be a total of six hours of input in the form of three two-hour blocks, each separated by a two-week gap to allow the family members (and, as it turned out, the prisoners) to do the 'homework' tasks that they were set. The three sessions progressed as follows with the intention to achieve a variety of goals and content (this content has been manualised and this manual is available on request).

Session 1: introduction and personal goals

The aim was to identify what experiences, skills and interests the prisoners currently have or have ever had in four areas:

- employment, training and education;
- sport, recreation, arts and culture;
- recovery groups, and other forms of peer activity; and
- volunteering and participation in a range of community activities.

The last part of the session was a guided session for family members to consider how they would explore:

- connections to these activities through their existing networks; and
- making completely new contacts to explore opportunities in each area.

The sessions also required individuals to undertake 'homework' to bring to the following session. The homework set for the family members at the end of session 1 included:

- Compile a list of contacts linked to the interests that the family member and their loved one came up with.
- Link those interests to the individuals, groups and organisations in their local area by drawing on their networks and discovering new information about their local communities.

The family members were asked to create a directory of all of those individuals and groups and to find out a bit more about them via websites, phone numbers and personal enquiries.

Session 2: establishing connections and developing connectors

Following a review of their initial experiences of making connections (either cold connections in the community or through mining existing networks), the group were asked to review what successes they had experienced and what barriers they had encountered. Following on from this, the main part of the session explored and taught the technique of asset mapping from the ABCD model, including the concept of the community connector. The teams of family members and participants were asked to come up with lists of activities and groups they were aware of in their local areas and to outline what their links were in terms of contacting each group. The last part of the session discussed what the key characteristics were for community connectors and how compatible family members saw themselves in this role. The session closed with family members being asked to assertively connect with the groups and activities identified following session 1 (homework for session 3), and to make 'live' some of those initial connections.

Session 3: assertive linkage and network development

Session 2 and the homework formed the basis for a recovery planning session in which action plans were developed in three sections – what could be done by the prisoners now to prepare; what could be done by the family members to build the relationships with external groups; and what the plans were for engagement on release. The session closed with reviews of the process and evaluation of the sessions. By the end of session 3, the aim was to have transitioned from each family working as a unit to the whole cohort working together. For this reason, we arranged a lunch after each session to allow the group to discuss what they had learned and how to address challenges and obstacles.

The primary aim was to help to build the links within family groups around shared purpose and positive collective goals and then to empower the family unit to work together to identify resources and assets that would match the long-term reintegration and personal growth needs of the prisoner. This is embedded within a strengths-based model that is relational and has as its objective the building of relationships with the local community.

Cohort 1 results

In the first cohort, there were a total of seven prisoners and 12 family members who took part in at least one session. The final session involved the seven prisoners and six family members who completed the evaluation. Overall, the final group consisted of nine males and four females, and the prisoners ranged in age from 35 to 47 and the family members from 25 to 79, with the latter group including parents, siblings and partners.

There were very high levels of wellbeing reported in the group using scales with ranges of 0–20, where higher scores represent better functioning. For psychological health the mean score was 17.0 (range of 6–20), for physical health the mean was 16.1 (range of 10–20) and for quality of life the mean was 15.8 (range of 10–20).

There was a very strong and consistent level of endorsement with all of the evaluation items that assessed attitudes about the training experience eliciting at least 4.5 out of 5. Participants were universally positive about the quality and relevance of the training, about how useful it will be to them, and the quality of training and support they received across the three sessions. We also used the same standardised evaluation tools from Texas Christian University (the Workshop Evaluation, or WEVAL) to assess perceived barriers to implementation. In contrast, to the positive perceptions about the training, with scores of between 1 and 5 (with lower scores representing low agreement), it was clear that the participants did not consider lack of time, lack of training or other priorities as barriers to implementing the training package.

Finally, in terms of the evaluation completed immediately after the last session, there is positive endorsement of the impact of the training on participants, who feel better equipped, understand the role of community connectors and who have accessed the relevant resources in the community, and who generally do not feel that it will not work nor that prisoners need better support. As such, this is a strong and consistent endorsement not only of the training, but also of its perceived efficacy and implementation. There were no participants who were not positive about the project or about their own experiences over the course of the sessions.

Qualitative feedback from the participants in the programme was extremely positive, in keeping with the quantitative findings above. One connector remarked that "you realise how important it is to be in contact with other people". One comment from another connector highlights the feeling of self-worth that they felt following their involvement with the programme where they describe feeling "like a small cog in the big picture of someone else's life. Every person counts and has a value." The accessible nature of the programme was also a key theme in the evaluation feedback, with workshops described as "well presented", "very interesting and relevant, but simplified" and that "everything said makes sense and if implemented should work". Perceived benefits and enjoyment of the programme were also documented with delivery described as "engaging" and overall positive feedback such as "I am sure everyone benefited from this session" and "absolutely loved this today".

From the staff perspective, there was also strong endorsement – feedback was overwhelmingly positive, with no negative comments made concerning the programme. The programme was described as "excellent … very interesting" and was praised for focusing on "what is important to the prisoners" and was therefore viewed as "more likely to have a positive impact". The rationale and conceptual framework for the programme was praised by staff: "[The programme had] excellent theoretical underpinning and the delivery was pitched ideally for the audience". The structure of the programme including its length and delivery across three workshops was also regarded positively, with the sessions described as "well planned and executed" as "the programme running over three sessions was perfect as it kept the prisoners interested and it was enough for the relatives in terms of travelling".

However, much more importantly, at a follow-up session, it transpired that one prisoner on release was able to get started in employment as a result of the connections made through the programme while a second had become actively involved in a youth football training programme, through a connection made during the training. As importantly, word spread among the prison staff and extremely positive feedback was received from staff who had witnessed any of the sessions or spoken to the prisoners who had taken part about their experiences.

The participants all recognised how the programme was intended to benefit them, describing hope, purpose, meaningful activities, and regulation of emotion as potential results of engaging with positive and meaningful networks and activities. Linked connections – people or groups connectors already knew – were described as easier to draw upon than unlinked connections, which demanded more research and social skills. In order to foster unlinked connections therefore the group were asked what qualities connectors might need to be successful. Responses included:

- Resilience. Confidence. Commitment.
- Being open. Patience. Enthusiasm.
- Communication skills.
- 'I've got something to offer' – no favours.
- Persistence. Thick-skin.
- Organisation.
- Learn from success and failures.

In conclusion, the programme was seen to have positive benefits (at least in the short term) for prisoners, their family/friendship units who engaged with the project, and prison staff who took part in the sessions. The theme of hope that emerged in the programme was particularly evident among the staff who were involved, who witnessed and contributed to the collective sense of purpose and active engagement of both the prisoners and the family members. On this basis, there was a strong commitment to running a second cohort of prisoners, making some adjustments, at least in part to incorporate some measure of hope in the evaluation process.

The second wave of connectors

One of the key actions taken in preparation for the second wave of connectors training was to conduct a workshop with the men who had taken part in the first phase as part of a review process for planning for the second wave. At the workshop, the perceptions remained favourable and it was evident that many of the participants were actively encouraging their peers to take part in the second cohort. As a result, demand among the men was much higher than for the first phase. Although there had been practical issues around payment of expenses for travel to volunteering opportunities and in obtaining the necessary Release On Temporary Licence (ROTL) to prepare for community engagement, enthusiasm was extremely high and it was at this session we were informed about some of the successes that had resulted from the initial training programme. Sufficient was the interest that we decided to alter the design of the programme to enable some of our new 'graduates' to participate in subsequent iterations as peer champions. This was partly about ensuring the sustainability of the project but also to ensure that it supported peer processes and peer ownership.

Further, there was considerable commitment and determination from the three probation staff who had clearly developed a sense of pride and ownership around the programme and who were very keen to take part in the second wave, and who suggested a number of additions and amendments. For this reason, it was agreed that the second cohort would have a much more active delivery component from the prison staff and a peer delivery component ensuring that the research team (which I led from Sheffield Hallam University) had a much smaller role.

In addition to the change in delivery team, there was also a decision to focus much more on social capital and hope. For this reason, we decided to incorporate a measure of social connections both at the start and at the end of the assessment procedure. Best et al (2014b) outlined the technique of social identity mapping in which sticky notes are headed with the names of groups that individuals belong to. For each group, the participant then notes the first name of each group member they regularly engage with. Then each name is colour coded (using sticky dots) to indicate whether the person is 'in recovery', a non-user, an occasional user or a problem user of illicit drugs or alcohol. This then creates a visualisation of the recovery capital available to the individual through their social networks. This was adapted to meet the rationale of attempting to build social capital (both bonding and bridging) so that we wanted a measure that would measure connections and the resulting links to social and community capital.

This involved combining the social identity mapping with a visualisation approach that has been widely used in education and addiction treatment called node-link mapping (Czuchry and

Dansereau, 2003). A dedicated map was created that attempted to reconcile a visualisation map for social identity (Best et al, 2014b; Haslam et al, 2017) with an asset mapping approach, and an example of what this map produced is shown in Figure 4.1.

This map attempts to combine the principles of node-link mapping as a visualisation tool for mapping access to social and community capital (the square boxes on the outer corners of the map) with social identity mapping that is described in Best et al (2014b). In this case, however, each contact is denoted for their active engagement with community resources so that the map constitutes both an overview of social identity and social connectedness, on the one hand, with a map of engagement with community assets on the other. As is evident from the

Figure 4.1: Social identity map and access to community capital from family member #1

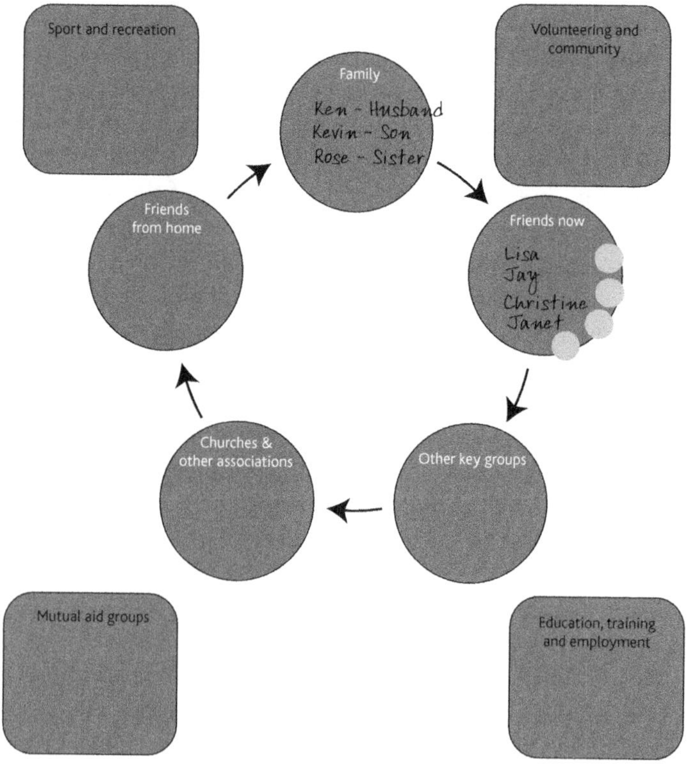

reproduced map from a family connector, they have no direct contacts with any of the core forms of community capital – mutual aid; education, training and employment, sport and recreation; and community groups and so all of the squares are blank. This person has a total of two networks consisting of seven individuals – and each of the people in the friendship group does have access to sport and recreational activities and so there are dots next to the name denoting their access to community resources. What this demonstrates is two things – first, that not only are people in prison lacking in access to community resources, but that this is also often the case for their family members. However, there is a seed of hope in that they have friends who can access community resources and this is critical to the thinking of this project.

Across all of the participants in the project, they perceived themselves to be members of an average of 4.1 groups (±1.4) and that they had contact with a total of 10.2 (±4.4) individuals. On average, there were a mean of 1.1 red dots (denoting substance users in their social network) per participant; 3.1 yellow dots (denoting links to sport and recreation groups); 2.1 green dots (denoting links to recovery and community groups); and 0.3 blue dots (denoting links to education, training and employment groups).[1] Thus, while there was typically some contact to sports, arts and recreation groups, there was almost no current engagement with groups linked to education, training or employment. In other words, the participants (both family members and prisoners) had a total of just over five connections to community resources. In terms of groups that they saw themselves to be part of, there was a mean of around one person linked to high risk behaviours.

Across the entire group, there were, however, a number of significant correlations in relation to social networks and connections:

- A greater number of links to drugs, alcohol and crime (red dots) was associated with markedly lower quality of life ($r=-0.74$, $p<0.05$).

- A greater number of green dots (links to community and recovery groups) was associated with better reported physical health ($r=0.78$, $p<0.01$).

This is consistent with a 'social cure' model (Jetten et al, 2012b) which suggests that greater links to pro-social groups are associated with better wellbeing and functioning. Although this is a limited and partial picture, it contributes to the suggestion that associations with using and offending groups is associated with poorer wellbeing while, in contrast, links to positive community assets were associated with higher levels of wellbeing. However, the most important point is that there is relatively limited access to community resources not only in the prisoner group but also in their families. Of the 41 groups and the 102 members identified by participants in the study, only around half (n=56) had any access to any of the forms of community resource (sport and recreation, recovery and community groups, and education, training and employment) with only one person having a link to the employment, training and education category. For this reason, we need to be clear that engagement in community groups is infrequent but not completely absent and that virtually all of the programme participants had some access to positive and pro-social groups – what we might refer to as 'secondary' community capital, as it could be derived through engagement with existing networks.

The evaluation results were also consistent with the first wave showing high levels of engagement and support and limited perceived barriers to effective implementation in the community. Positive scores were recorded for hope, although this was only measured at the end point in the evaluation. A second consequence of the project was the sense of active participation and collective commitment in the cohort of those training and those trained – there was a genuine sense of a growth in hope and belief that effective community engagement would be possible on release and that there were individual and collective strengths to build on. One of the most powerful vindications of the programme was the faith that participants developed in it. The strength-based model is salutogenic, generating wellbeing among participants and creating a sense of collective purpose and collective identity.

The project has also led to a growing sense of confidence and collaboration among the staff and prisoner volunteers participating in the project. The team of probation staff, despite resource limitations in the prison, have become extremely committed to the project and are active champions for it while the inclusion of prison volunteers has meant that recruitment of future cohorts of participants is significantly enhanced.

Implications from the community connectors work

In this chapter, the principles of ABCD and assertive linkage have been applied in a prison context with the evaluation data from both waves of the project providing clear evidence of the engagement and commitment of all three of the participating groups – staff in the prison, prisoners and family members who have worked together to support each other to identify and build on community connections. While this work remains a pilot project there are four core areas that merit consideration in the review of this work:

1. community connections and reciprocal community development;
2. the contagion of hope;
3. positive criminology; and
4. from connections to pro-social groups and activities to desistance and recovery.

Community connections and reciprocal community development

The key point about this work is the importance of establishing and building on positive connections to support pro-social activities and the engagement with positive community resources that can provide access to social capital and membership of positive and pro-social networks. The underlying assumption for which evidence is provided in this paper is that many prisoners about to leave prison (and perhaps more surprisingly their family members) lack strong social networks, and are particularly low in bridging capital to pro-social groups that have access to community resources. This is the justification for the Kirkham Family Connectors work as it successfully identified a gap in the resources available to successfully affect the transition back into the community.

Although it is far too early at the time of writing to comment on the long-term impact of the connectors project, it has created viable pathways to community connections. In both cohorts of the pilot study, offenders and their family members were asked to identify skills, interests and passions and then to come up with ways of linking into these groups and activities, both by tapping into existing social capital and connections and, where this was not possible, by tracking down resources in the local community that contact could be made with. In each of the cohorts run to date, the family members were able to do exactly that and it was a bonus that some of the prisoners were sufficiently engaged and inspired that they also did what they could in tracking down resources from inside prison. Indeed, we changed the programme in the first wave to give the prisoners a far more prominent role, based on their levels of engagement and enthusiasm.

This is not only a vindication of the training but also an important feasibility step in ensuring that this is not too complex or demanding a task, and to ensure that the programme could be widely implemented with relatively small levels of resource. In both cohorts, all of the families did the 'homework' tasks and successfully managed to identify and engage with community assets. So the second issue of feasibility was also answered in the affirmative – with relatively small amounts of exposure to training and support, family members were able to access community resources and were able to link those assets to the interests and the needs of the prisoners.

There is an additional component part of the process that is important – we know from the evidence that there is a need for family restoration as the gaps caused by the time spent in prison has the ability to reduce trust and weaken social bonds (Wolff and Draine, 2004). What became apparent was that the process of working together on the tasks was positive in terms of building and reaffirming the relationships within the families – the collective process of working on the identification of skills and then applying that to establish community connections provided a shared sense of goals and purpose that were reported in the evaluations to be positive and important.

The social contagion of hope

When the project was first proposed, there were three primary barriers: anxiety from the probation team in the prison about monitoring and measuring risk associated with the project (and related governance issues); concerns that family members would not be willing to mix and work with each other; and concerns that there would be low uptake of and engagement with the project.

The first concern was expressed by the three probation officers who had concerns about both the selection of clients and their subsequent engagement in the community. Indeed, it was primarily the commitment of the governor that provided the reassurance to push the project through in spite of these objections. As a result of their professionalism, all three of the probation officers committed to the project and were instrumental in ensuring that sufficient prisoners were recruited to each of the cohorts and they actively participated in the training programme, and they developed a risk protocol to ensure that no prisoners or family members were at risk during the project. It was the training events that fundamentally transformed their perceptions about the project – they rapidly became champions for the programme and all three now are vocal advocates and each one of them has a strong sense of pride and commitment in the project. Their experience of working with families and clients in effect 're-connected' them with the feelings of pride and commitment about why they had joined the profession in the first place, and about the possibilities for supporting effective reintegration for the participants.

This collective sense of commitment also influenced the family members. The anxiety expressed in advance was that family members would stick to their family groups and there would be little interaction between family groups as a result of stigma, shame and suspicion. In each of the completed cohorts, there was some evidence of this in the first session, but this rapidly dissipated and by the second session in each cohort there was a strong commitment to the project, and session 3 in each cohort saw a strong sense of group commitment emerging.

The final concern was that there would be low uptake and engagement – although managing process meant that there were some delays in the first cohort, partly as we established processes and protocols, this had disappeared by the second cohort, as word of mouth spread through the prisoner community. The fact that several of the initial cohort were willing to be trainers in the second cohort and were convinced about its merits spread rapidly through the prisoner cohort and demand for participation was high. As already outlined, when the families were recruited, they were active participants in the project, as were, less predictably, the prisoners.

So why should we have experienced such positive engagement and manage to overcome all three of the barriers? The answer is in the title of the book – the contagion of hope. What we managed to tap into was a process that inspired relational engagement, commitment to the process and to each other and, crucially, an emerging belief that the prisoner would have a positive future on release from prison. This transmitted through the group as a group, and the role differences between participants was diminished through collective engagement and endeavour. Following the first cohort, one participant reported to me that the project was the first time in 13 years in prison that someone had asked them what they were good at. This is the fundamental principle of community connections projects: they are based on strengths and hope, and the process requires shared engagement and shared commitment. One consequence of this, anecdotally, was stronger relationships with the family member, as trust along with hope spread through the group and broke down many negative experiences and expectations.

Positive criminology

Although the concept of positive criminology dates back to the start of the 20th century, it has gained momentum in recent years with the development of the 'Good Lives Model', originally proposed by Ward and Stewart (2003) and captured in a recent edited volume by Ronel and Segev (2015). Essentially, it is a model that is strengths-based and focuses on rehabilitation and life transformations, and is linked to the positive psychology movement. This is part of a wider transition in academic thinking and research that is linked to human services and vulnerable populations and that has its origins in positive psychology and criminology within the social sciences and in fields as disparate as restorative justice, therapeutic jurisprudence (both related to legal practice) and the recovery movements in both mental health and drug and alcohol addiction. This shift in approach is based on a recognition that there are wider issues around social justice, community cohesion and individual quality of life and wellbeing that can be meshed through such approaches.

Based on a humanistic tradition of wellbeing as a holistic quality of experience that involves not only the principal but those that surround him or her, there is a recognition that the support of vulnerable populations needs to be relationally focused, community based and sustainable. This is not to suggest that there is no place for a traditional 'clinical' approach but that it is not always necessary and it will never be sufficient to address much larger questions of inclusion and participation in the rights and values of communities. Community focused approaches do not neglect individuals but attempt to improve the lives of individuals by focusing on the group and the community as the place where interventions should take place. This is because the community is the level at which hope can spread and structural changes that can support and enable change can happen. The positive criminology tradition provides that frame for both 'do no harm' but also encourages academics not to be detached observers but 'community activists' who can both chart successes and inspire others to believe that positive change is realistic and sustainable.

The translation of connections to desistance and recovery

This chapter started with an overview of the literature around desistance and the recognition that there are key interpersonal factors (including but not restricted to informal social control) that inform the process of desistance. However, desistance research, while recognising the importance of relationships (in particular marriage) and social networks (antisocial peers are a key risk factor in the Risk Need Responsivity model; Andrews and Bonta, 1998), has had relatively little engagement with the idea that groups and communities can be actively engaged as predictors of reintegration and rehabilitation. While the ABCD model has become increasingly common in the application of recovery policy in the UK for substance use and for mental health, there is much less evidence that the same approach has been applied to rehabilitation and crime. The recognition of the importance of family has not extended to questions of shared activity and the idea that family members can constitute a valuable resource, and that collectively family members are stakeholders who generally want to be and are willing to be mobilised and supported. Crucially, this is not a 'zero sum game' and the idea is that not only does the offender benefit from the linkage process, but so also do all of the members of the family, first by increased positive engagement with the offender (to generate bonding capital) but also by increasing their own connections in the community (through bridging and linking capital).

Future directions

A cautionary note is important at this point – this is not a panacea. Not all offenders have ongoing contact with their families and for others, the family may play a part in their offending or the problems associated with it (substance use, domestic violence, trauma and mental health problems). Therefore a degree of caution is required in planning for generalisability and widespread application. These were very real concerns and discussions in the planning and implementation of the pilot projects and their importance should not be overlooked. Yet what the study has demonstrated is the feasibility of this approach and the willingness of three groups – prison staff, prisoners and their families – to come together with a common purpose and to work collectively (and without professional boundaries and barriers) to create pathways to meaningful activities and in doing so to generate a positive collective identity and a sense of sustainable hope. Much work is needed to test what impact this has in the longer term following release for participants (and for their family members) but the signs are positive and encouraging, and there is much benefit in the process and its impact on increasing community cohesion in prisons. It is clear that participation in the programme improves relationships between prisoners and their families, and also between prisoners and the prison staff involved in the programme.

As with much of the work described in this book, the implications extend significantly beyond the immediate topic to broader issues of connections and their impact on social identity and self-perception, based on the idea that sustainable change is a social contract between the offender or drug user and the community (including human services and the structures they support). In the next chapter, the focus will switch to a four-year project (that is ongoing) to creating sustainable change in the community in Sheffield and the surrounding area, with the latter half of the chapter focusing on change in Doncaster, a slightly smaller city around 15 miles to the east of Sheffield.

Key lessons

- Families' needs have largely been neglected in a prison context and the recent Farmer Report (Farmer, 2017) in the UK has emphasised the need for greater involvement of families to support the wellbeing of prisoners.

- The transition from prison to the community is a major risk for recidivism and relapse often triggered by lack of access to the kinds of capital (houses, jobs, support networks) that can support sustainable change.

- The Kirkham Family Connectors project was designed in partnership with staff at HMP Kirkham, a Category D open prison, to support families become part of the process of building bridges in the communities that offenders will return to.

- The programme is a partnership between prisoners, family members and prison staff to learn the principles of ABCD, assertive linkage and community connections.
- The first two waves yielded high levels of engagement and hope across all three groups and a strong team and community ethos was generated as a result, with improved relationships between families and prisoners, but also between prison staff and the other two groups.
- The preliminary evaluation from the first two waves of participants suggested high levels of approval and the emergence of a sense of hope, with increased demand for the programme once word had spread through the prison population.
- Particularly important was the sense that the programme both reinvigorated a belief in their professional values among the probation staff and a feeling of direction and purpose in the prisoners and families. This is a consequence of adopting and communicating a strengths-based approach that is future-oriented and hope-based.
- While there are not yet outcome data from the study, it is clear that this strengths-based approach has considerable potential for building bridges and for creating circles of support around prisoners to support their return to the community.

Note

1 Red dots denote that this individual was involved with drinking, drug use or crime; yellow dots denote connections to sport and recreation groups; green dots denote access to recovery or community groups; blue dots denote access to employment, education or training resources.

5

Recovery, research and communities: Sheffield Addiction Recovery Research Group and recovery cities

Background and rationale

In my work in both the UK and Australia, I have been involved in establishing recovery research groups – first, the Recovery Academy in the UK and, second, Recovery Academy Australia (RAA) based in Melbourne. The work of the Recovery Academy is described in detail in a special issue of the *Journal of Groups in Addiction and Recovery* (JGAR), which was subsequently published as an edited book (Roth and Best, 2013). The Recovery Academy was a forum that was established to showcase recovery research and innovation in a very applied and practical way. The annual conference was the focal point of the Recovery Academy and was explicitly designed to influence both addiction practitioners and policy makers in Scotland and more widely across the UK. The Recovery Academy was entirely independent and run without external funding or support, although it worked closely with the Scottish Drugs Recovery Consortium (SDRC) and with the organisers of the UK Recovery Walks.

A very similar model was implemented in Melbourne, in Australia, attempting to replicate some of the successes of the UK version but starting from a much more limited policy base. Australia, at the time of the RAA inception in 2011, had a very strong policy and practice commitment to a harm reduction model and the recovery approach was seen by some as a challenge to this approach. In partnership with the Self-Help Addiction Recovery Centre (SHARC), an initially small group of academics met to discuss raising awareness of recovery and support for partnership and working together. A similar process was initiated with an annual conference but on this occasion it was supplemented by a recovery walk, held in Melbourne in 2012, which attracted considerable media attention and provided a mechanism for raising awareness and promoting recovery as a social movement. As visible recovery was at a much earlier stage in Australia, our activities were primarily around events, such as the recovery walk in Melbourne and the conference, to raise awareness of recovery and to provide a sense of collective identity and purpose for those who were able and willing to champion a visible public face for recovery.

On this basis, and with two colleagues from Melbourne, Melinda Beckwith and Ana-Maria Bliuc, we wrote about recovery as a pre-figurative political movement (Beckwith et al, 2016). The basic argument of this research paper was that recovery is not only a personal experience but also has two primary interpersonal formulations. Recovery can also be considered as something that happens between people as part of a social contagion where people are both inspired to attempt recovery and learn how to manage the process through observing inspirational people who are already there. However, there is also a third sense of recovery as a social movement with the aim to celebrate the achievement of recovery and to promote its goals. This sense of movement was described in the paper as something that can create collective support and hope, and the sense of identity associated with being part of something vibrant, positive and exciting. One of the most established mechanisms for promoting this public model has been through recovery walks as a form of celebration.

The idea of a recovery walk, as done repeatedly now in the US, UK and Australia, begins with five objectives:

1. To help individuals celebrate the achievement of recovery.
2. To inspire others who are not yet at that point to believe that recovery is possible and that they can achieve it, because here is a living embodiment of recovery.

3. To provide a 'public face' to recovery as a challenge to stereotyped and negative views.
4. To create a platform for political lobbying and to demonstrate the scale and power of the recovery community to manage and support change.
5. To make visible the power of the recovery community as an asset in the local community.

The idea of a pre-figurative political movement is for a community led or 'ground-up' model of realising political strength through a shared and collective identity to achieve particular goals, and that does not accept professional orthodoxies or be restricted by them. The other crucial point of recovery as a social movement is that it is not restricted to a single philosophy or to a particular population. The recovery walks have typically been inclusive events involving people who have achieved recovery through a range of different methods (such as 12-step mutual aid and TCs) but also different populations. One of the most engaging and appealing aspects of recovery celebration events has been the coming together of various populations – people in recovery, their families, people who work in the field with no lived experience, researchers and policy makers, and any other members of the community. They are typically open and inclusive events.

There is a key point here about recovery as a social movement – it requires the engagement of multiple populations who come together to form a coalition of recovery support. This creates the basis and foundations for active engagement with policy makers and practitioners, and allows the emergence of the recovery model to subvert the orthodoxy of treatment delivery. This does not mean that community and peer-based activities are alternatives to treatment but rather that they can enhance and supplement that model. Once again, there is a critical role for peers in this process of transformation.

Sheffield Addiction Recovery Research Group

It was from this foundation that we attempted to establish a local partnership base for recovery and recovery research in Sheffield.

Following a series of initial discussions in 2014 to 2015, Sheffield Addiction Recovery Research Group (SARRG) was established as a partnership initially between Sheffield Hallam University, Sheffield University, Sheffield City Council and its Drug and Alcohol Commissioning Team, Sheffield Alcohol Support Services (SASS) and Sheffield Health and Social Care Trust (SHSC).

Initially, the aim was to identify existing research activity that was relevant to recovery in the city and to build a platform for partnership and participation around recovery. However, this in essence was a mapping exercise with three existing groups or activities providing a strong foundation for the proposed partnership.

The first of these was Service User Reference Group (SURG), a user representation group that was coordinated through the treatment commissioners in the City Council, provided a valuable interface between service users and providers and had coordinated Recovery Month activities in Sheffield each September. Sheffield City Council had shown an ongoing commitment to recovery processes through Recovery Month as an annual event including participation processes for family members and an ongoing peer and volunteer scheme.

The second initiative was based on a Public Patient Involvement (PPI) panel that had been developed in the city by staff at Sheffield University for other health issues, and who were looking to apply this to alcohol and drug research. This is a key initiative about user participation in research design and development, not just in planning and bidding for research funds but also in ensuring that participants remain active stakeholders throughout the research process including the dissemination phase.

The third key foundation stone for this work was the annual conference run by SASS, a local non-governmental organisation (NGO) that had demonstrated a strong and lasting commitment to recovery and to evidence-based practice in the work they did across the city.

It is also important to acknowledge the support from my own organisation, Sheffield Hallam University, which provided both financial support and flexibility around staff time in supporting the project. This provided the organisational foundations for the initial feasibility meetings and there was an enthusiastic response from a range of stakeholders.

Launching SARRG and establishing an agenda

Sheffield Hallam University has hosted a social justice week event over a number of years as a means of actively engaging the general public in issues around human rights and social justice. In 2015, this provided the platform to launch SARRG. The vision was to create a peer-led group to support recovery-oriented activities and to undertake research and action focused on enhancing recovery from addiction. The Group formed a coalition of people in recovery, services, commissioners, academics and the wider community representing differing pathways to recovery, actively supporting the recovery community, promoting events, and providing help and expert advice to groups asking for support. SARRG's vision was to make Sheffield the UK's foremost recovery city, providing a model of advanced recovery research and action for others to follow, building on a diverse range of existing champions and activities in the city and providing a common banner to bring people together to support recovery pathways.

The basic idea was to have four events a year – a conference, a recovery event to celebrate Recovery Month, a music festival and a Christmas meal. The event for the annual celebration of recovery was a bike ride to take place each September in the Peak District to encourage sporting activity and collaborative team work. This was meant to be a visible celebration of the possibility of recovery and so all of the participants wore recovery t-shirts in the recovery colour of purple to promote collective identity and to promote a positive and healthy image of recovery.

As outlined above, the aim of the bike ride was to create a collective sense of positive identity and achievement among those taking part, to demonstrate that recovery is possible and can be fun, to challenge exclusionary and stigmatising attitudes and beliefs, and to generate political capital. However, there is another crucial purpose around the social identity component of engagement and participation which relates to the idea of a 'recovery coalition'.

Although White (2009) has argued that the primary 'carriers' of the contagion of recovery are people with lived experience, recovery must be inclusive and participatory, and effective recovery systems require advocates and champions beyond those who are able to act as carriers of the contagion of recovery. While lived experience provides the forum for social learning (for example, Moos, 2007), the social control component can also involve families and other key stakeholders. Two key groups in this coalition are academics, who can provide the evidence and who have a responsibility to act as 'research activists', and a diverse range of professionals who can break down the barriers between community activities and professional interventions, and for whom building those bridges to recovery communities is essential in establishing viable recovery systems of care. Their practice needs to support the inclusive, holistic and personalised components of connections and personal growth.

For this reason, it was incredibly gratifying that the coalition included a number of professionals (some of whom may well have had lived experience) as well as researchers and academics from both Sheffield universities, and a range of family members and community supporters (including a police inspector). One of the core objectives of this partnership is to move towards a recovery-oriented system of care. In a summary of the evidence for the SAMHSA, Sheedy and Whitter outlined the key characteristics of a recovery-oriented system as:

1. Person-centred
2. Inclusive of family and other ally involvement
3. Individualised and comprehensive services across the lifespan
4. Systems anchored in the community
5. Continuity of care
6. Partnership–consultant relationships
7. Strength-based
8. Culturally responsive
9. Responsiveness to personal belief systems
10. Commitment to peer recovery support services
11. Integrated services
12. System-wide education and training

13. Inclusion of the voices and experiences of recovering individuals and their families
14. Ongoing monitoring and evaluation
15. Evidence driven
16. Research based
17. Adequately and flexibly funded

While many of the key elements here have already been discussed, the key ideas here are around partnership–consultant relationships, systems anchored in the community, integrated services, inclusion of the voices of recovering individuals and their families, and strengths-based working.

In many ways, SARRG epitomised this model by trying to create a model where public events – like the Recovery Month Celebrations, the summer music festival (in conjunction with SASS) and the conference – all attempted to build a city-wide partnership that had a range of stakeholders (including but not led by academics) at its core, with a view that this would expand and develop as the recovery community (and the city) evolved. Peer involvement is at the heart of this model but the rationale is inclusive and designed to engage multiple stakeholders.

The fundamental aim here is academic activism where deploying (and generating) research evidence is a core part of the process of building a knowledge base. All of the events were free and did not attempt to specify whether participants were in recovery or why they were interested in being engaged. The purpose was to increase awareness that recovery is possible, to celebrate and disseminate the successes of recovery (a form of social contagion of hope) and engage in a range of activities that challenged negative stereotypes and increased community inclusion. In the principles of recovery-oriented systems of care (ROSC), inclusion features on three separate occasions and one of the core aims of these kinds of events is to generate community capital through building the three kinds of social capital specified by Putnam (2000):

- *bonding capital* through the celebration of success, in settings where people can be proud of their own successes and can support and laud the efforts of others;

- *bridging capital* by building links between people in recovery and family members on the one hand, and community activists, academics and a range of professionals on the other, under the common umbrella of the recovery movement; and
- *linking capital* by providing those who are socially marginalised and excluded (primarily people in recovery but also family members) with access to resources in the community through links to professionals and members of local community groups and activities, that they otherwise may not know about or have access to.

In this way, there was an attempt not only to make Sheffield a centre of knowledge and expertise about recovery processes and activities but also to provide a forum for exchange and growth. In the next section, we explore how this partnership translated into an asset mapping process for Sheffield and to a formal research study.

A partnership basis for asset mapping as a learning process

As has been outlined previously, one of the key approaches to building community resources to support the multiple pathways to desistance and recovery has been through ABCD, both to identify resources in communities and to then link to them. Based on this model, a PhD studentship was arranged between Sheffield Hallam University and SASS, which had been a prominent and consistent supporter of SARRG from its inception and which hosted one of SARRG's four annual events, the summer music festival.

For the PhD, we recruited a student, Beth Collinson, who had graduated from Sheffield Hallam University and already had strong connections in the city. The aim of the PhD was to look at gender differences in social networks and social capital, and how connections are used to support recovery pathways and recovery journeys. The research questions for the PhD were:

1. How well do existing measures capture the three elements of recovery capital?

2. How would we go about developing adequate measures that assess recovery resources at the social and community level, and establish norms for those measures?
3. How do we test this approach with populations at different stages of their recovery journeys and map changes in recovery capital in those populations?
4. What are the key parameters of community capital and how are they related to stigma and exclusion, and how can we demonstrate impact of community capital on personal recovery pathways?
5. In each of the above areas, are there differences between the recovery journeys of men and women?

The project focused on the Alcohol Recovery Community, which is one project among many supported by SASS (and includes a residential rehabilitation unit). The Alcohol Recovery Community is a peer support service designed to help people get through all recovery stages, whether they have completed clinical treatment or are looking to take that initial step towards alcohol reduction. The service was designed to provide hope and to offer choice through a range of recovery support opportunities and so it was a perfect location for a community engagement project. SASS is a well-established recovery NGO that offers specialist services and drop-in facilities for people overcoming alcohol problems.

The first mapping exercise was conducted on 26 July 2016 as part of the SARRG meeting cycle in the Jesus Centre in Sheffield, with around 40 people taking part from a range of local organisations and groups. The initial identification of assets provided a diverse range of support services available in the four core areas of: sport and recreation; education, training and employment; community engagement and volunteering; and mutual aid.

The overall asset map is shown in Figure 5.1.

One of the strengths of an asset based visualisation approach like this is that it is creative and can be amended to suit the needs of the participants and in Figure 5.1 it can be seen that there is an additional 'hub' for professional services that are seen as central to the process of asset mapping. This is consistent with

Figure 5.1: Overall asset map for Sheffield

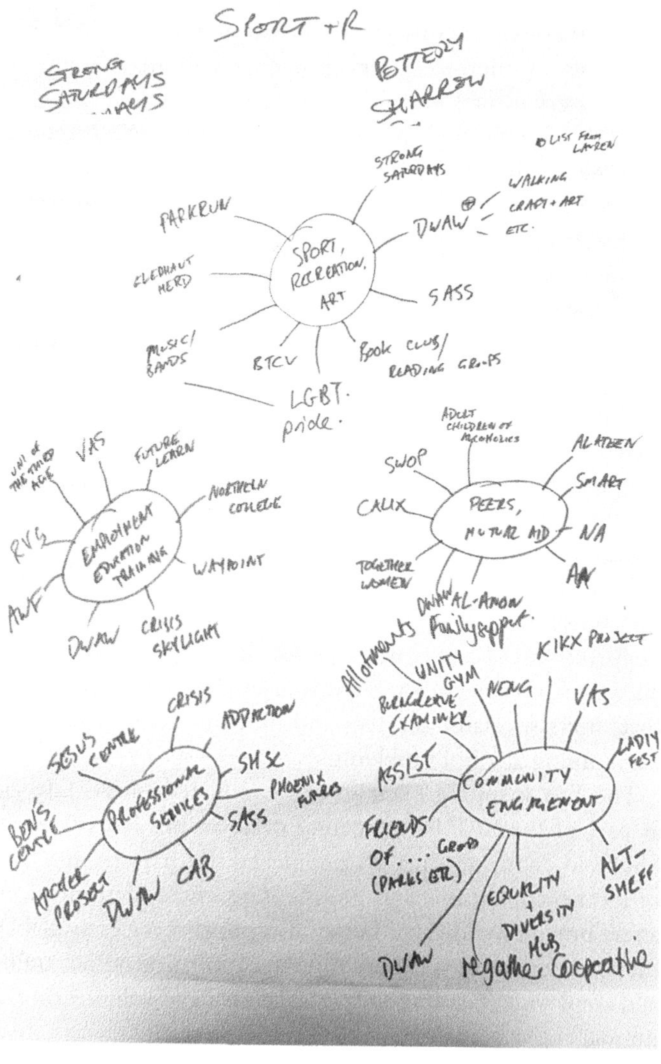

the inclusivity theme for this work and in particular the idea that recovery is best supported through a coalition of partners that is not restricted to peers, and draws on a more diverse set of networks and assets.

The richness of the exercise is in the engagement and creativity of the participants first in identifying appropriate assets and then in identifying community connectors to link into those assets. However, the PhD student wanted to assess in greater depth how individuals engaged with the assets and so also measured the accessibility, affordability and connections/networks afforded by each type of group to keep a dynamic model of engagement as part of the process.

This is a good example of how the original work by the ABCD Institute has created a framework that can be adapted for other purposes, whether they are academic or more practical. Participants were asked to rate each asset on four dimensions:

1. Accessibility
2. Affordability
3. Connectedness
4. Networks

The purpose of this exercise was to start to record systematically (and visually) how each participant was able to engage effectively with each of the assets identified. It is done as a visualisation so that it is accessible and meaningful to participants and allows us to quickly code the strengths of each group that the person engages with. It is critical for recovery research that it is inclusive and accessible to research participants, and that the results and outputs can be directly translated to supporting individuals and groups in their recovery journeys.

Therefore, in the example given, there is high affordability for the SMART group (it is free) but the location is not great and so the rating for accessibility is markedly lower. This participant has also rated the group as high in terms of connections offered. This part of the project aims to move beyond mapping as an exercise in creating a directory to one that is interactive and allows feedback and reflection from those who actively engage with each resource.

In the doctoral study, Beth is measuring what long-term impact engagement has had on the recovery outcomes of the participants – with a particular emphasis on assessing gender differences. However, it is critical to note that the asset mapping component is not only about producing an output, it is also about the process of active engagement of groups in generating the asset maps and then working with them to make real connections and to establish viable pathways into longer-term recovery. This is an iterative process that has shaped future work in this area but has also built connections and built alliances of champions to support the process. Part of the purpose of undertaking asset mapping is to generate a coalition of potential community connectors.

Furthermore, this work in effect paved the way for the Community Connectors project that is described in more detail in Chapter 6. I now offer a brief overview of this connectors work before concluding this work in relation to an exciting initiative that has taken place 20 miles away from Sheffield in the city of Doncaster. It is essential that there is a 'legacy' component in these recovery initiatives to ensure that the commitment and engagement that is generated does not dissipate and that the process continues through ongoing support for local communities and local activities.

The SARRG initiative attempted to actively engage the local community in recovery research – the organisation and development of it, its integration and application in the city and also in maximising its impact for the local community. This is a generative and developmental process and one of the key successes was the establishment and growth of partnerships and trust that led not only to a PhD studentship but also to culture change to participation and sharing and to developing innovative methods to support community engagement.

There are essentially three levels at which the establishment of SARRG offered relational opportunities – first, at the level of organisations, with both of the universities in Sheffield actively engaged in a partnership that also included the City Council, the NHS Trust and a number of NGOs. Second, there were significant opportunities for building relationships between individuals and teams within professional organisations (a clear form of linking capital) that formed alliances and improved pathways in the city. The third level is bridging capital, which was particularly relevant to the mentors and peer champions in the delivery services who were afforded opportunities to get actively involved in a range of higher level activities and opportunities. This is both linking and bridging capital as new connections were made inside organisations and links were established with a much broader range of groups and associations that helped to build recovery capital in Sheffield and to establish new forms of community capital.

This notion of establishing bonds and relationships is now discussed in the neighbouring city of Doncaster, where two initiatives – Recovery College and recovery cities – have evolved from an initial partnership with the local NHS Trust.

Doncaster: a recovery city?

Together with its surrounding suburbs and settlements, the town forms part of the Metropolitan Borough of Doncaster, which had a mid-2016 estimated population of 306,400, of whom around 160,000 live in the urban area. Although it has pockets of affluence, Doncaster is largely an area of high deprivation and this poses significant public health challenges.

My involvement with Doncaster has largely been based on engagement with the drug and alcohol services, Aspire, which is a part of the Rotherham, Doncaster And South Humber NHS Trust (RDASH), for whom I have done a number of conference talks and training workshops over the years. In 2017, I became an Honorary Research Fellow at the Trust, a position I was delighted to accept, and this has grown through two emerging initiatives that are both concerned with aspects of community connectedness and social inclusion. The staff and services in Doncaster have shown a significant commitment to innovative practice and have a strong recovery focus that we have been able to build on for the projects described next.

Recovery College

The aim of the Recovery College was to create a platform for building research, education and training around addiction recovery both in community and in criminal justice settings. However, there was a particular aspiration for these training, wellbeing and development needs to be met through a partnership focused on the wellbeing of participants.

Three organisations – Sheffield Hallam University, RDASH and Spectrum (a primary health care provider in both the community and prison sectors) – agreed on a strategic partnership to provide developmental and training events three times a year to support all of those involved in delivering recovery-oriented interventions and activities. Thus, there was a top-down component to this initiative, which involved senior leaders and opinion formers in the three organisations coming together to support this activity and to put together a strategic vision for how this would work. However, there is also significant capacity building work for staff and volunteers in each of the participating organisations that creates bonding and linking capital (Putnam, 2000) and is embedded in an inclusive notion of strengths-based and relational working. Each of the events showcases both work that is done inside each organisation and outside speakers who are engaged in innovative applied activities in each of these areas.

There is also an explicit objective in relation to ROSC (Sheedy and Whitter, 2009) with regards to worker wellbeing. While the aim of the Recovery College is to promote recovery-oriented evidence-based practice, it is also designed to be inclusive and to fulfil the requirement of partnership working. That means that there has to be an assumption that the journey to recovery applies to the workforce and to volunteers just as much as it does to clients. This is not only because a significant proportion of the workforce may be in recovery themselves, but also because recovery is characterised as a shared and relational phenomenon (Best, 2014) in which each person should benefit and grow from participating in recovery-oriented activities, increasing personal, social and community capital. There is considerable emotional labour involved in working in early recovery and this can take a toll on the workforce (for example, Butler et al, 2018). In contrast, the rewards of supporting recovery and the wider implications for the community can be extremely positive and beneficial for the workforce.

Furthermore, there is also good evidence that the capacity to provide a meaningful therapeutic alliance requires wellbeing on the part of the worker. In a paper based on an online survey of 208 drug and alcohol workers in Victoria, Australia, Best et al (2016) found that around one quarter of staff had psychological health levels below that reported by the average client on admission to treatment services. However, the key finding was that workers who reported lower levels of psychological health and poorer quality of life also reported lower levels of therapeutic optimism. In other words, when staff are struggling with their own wellbeing they are less able to engage fully in the kinds of positive therapeutic relationships that are necessary to support their clients, and to build recovery-oriented relationships for change.

Thus, the aim of the Recovery College is not only to provide a forum for staff to learn about recovery and the underlying evidence base but also for the leaders of each organisation to learn about and support the health and wellbeing of those involved. This is particularly crucial for those who are volunteering or mentoring having formerly been involved in services as clients. One of the core objectives is to look to provide support to 'experts by experience' and to identify what their learning and support needs are in building longer-term recovery pathways. Building on these principles of relational and strengths-based working, the Recovery College is a forum for providing linkages and offering a space for growth and shared learning. This is predicated on the assumption that personal capital grows in tandem with social and community capital, and that the Recovery College will create stronger workers and also generate community assets and resources.

Recovery cities

In part, this idea is taken from the developing work around restorative justice and the evolution of this approach into the broader ideas of restorative practice. Among the most eminent writers in this area is Howard Zehr, who has defined restorative justice as 'a process to involve those who have a stake in a specific offense to collectively identify and address harms, needs and obligations in order to heal and put things as right as possible' (Zehr and Gohar, 2002: 40). Restorative justice is as much a system of ideals and principles underlying practices as a system of practices; it is, as Gavrielides has articulated, an 'ethos' (Gavrielides, 2007: 139; 2014). This way of thinking about the potential ramifications of restorative principles has led to their application in fields as wide as governance and education, with an ethos of inclusion and participation that is entirely consistent with the recovery model outlined in this book and the method of community connections. Both on theoretical and practical levels, restorative justice and recovery have embraced interpersonal change as an intrapersonal, holistic, and relational phenomenon (Llewellyn et al, 2013; Best and Laudet, 2010) and they rely upon mechanisms within broader communities to leverage change at a personal level by providing forums in which positive change is made a reality through strengths-building exercises.

Thus, the idea of a recovery city draws on and develops the ideas taken forward in a parallel area. While both Hull and Leeds in the UK have embraced the idea of restorative cities, perhaps the most established example is from Canberra in Australia where, in 2016, the Australian Capital Territory Legislative Assembly initiated the works towards the declaration of Canberra as a restorative city with a commitment to exploring and implementing creative solutions to shared problems using restorative processes. One of the core goals of this initiative was to ensure that restorative principles were increasingly seen as a viable alternative to traditional responses to conflict and other forms of harmful behaviour.

The notion here is that there is some form of 'top-down' policy and procedural commitment to a new way of doing things that informs the ethos and philosophy of both practitioners and citizens to increase inclusion and to give a voice to victims and other excluded groups. For Canberra the aim was to create a 'Restorative, Compassionate and Honest City; A Democratic City' through changing beliefs, culture, norms and relationships at all levels throughout the city (ACT Law Reform Advisory Council, 2017). Among the local recommendations was the need for a restorative framework which meant that, across all organisations, there was a need to improve relationship skills, improve skills for conflict resolution, and also to ensure that institutional frameworks and legislative provisions are sufficient to support these changes. This involved generating not only high level commitment from policy makers and legislators, but also creating a visible consensus and engagement in the process. Among the underlying principles were transparent decision making, 'the promotion of a best practice human rights culture at a government and institutional level' (ACT Law Reform Advisory Council, 2017: 9), and a commitment to natural justice.

The same principles and rules were not universalised across all of the restorative cities – it is a loose coalition, based on sharing ideas and experiences and evidence. Thus, cities sign up to an ethos and a set of principles rather than strict rules for membership. A similar model applies to the concept of recovery cities, based on a shared set of values and a commitment to principles of social justice and learning from an emerging evidence base of practices to promote inclusion and tackle stigma. The aim of recovery cities is to make recovery visible, to celebrate it and to create a safe environment supportive to recovery. As with restorative cities, the aim was to use the principles of recovery to support broader aims of inclusion and fairness throughout the community. The aims for recovery cities are:

- to make whole cities into 'therapeutic landscapes for recovery' – places that support recovery changes and have inclusive approaches to reintegration;
- to use recovery as social inclusion as a starting point for challenging wider social exclusion and actively engaging marginalised populations; and
- to create a 'connected communities' model that challenges social exclusion and so health inequalities.

These inclusive cities are not only beneficial for the person in recovery, but also for the community and city as a whole. In this respect, this is a meso and macro version of the work done with reciprocal community development (and outlined in Chapters 2 and 3). In Table 5.1, we have outlined what Best and Colman (2018) have indicated are the key areas for defining a recovery city.

Table 5.1: Components of an inclusive city

Theoretical component of an inclusive city	Operational elements
Connectedness and social cohesion	• Peer support and involvement • Community support and involvement • Mutual aid • Relationships with others • Establishing bridging and linking capital
Hope about the future	• Belief in the possibility of recovery • Champion visibility of recovery and celebrate success • Motivation to change • Hope-inspiring relationships • Positive thinking and valuing success • Having dreams and aspirations
Promoting a recovery identity around social inclusion and social participation	• Rebuilding/redefining a positive sense of identity • Challenging exclusionary labels and practices – work with housing services, employment agencies, and so on, to challenge exclusionary processes and structures
Meaning	• Meaningful life and social roles: access to meaningful jobs and accessible recovery housing • Contribute and give back to the community • Opportunities for volunteering and access to community resources
Empowerment and strength-based	• Personal responsibility • Control over life • Focus on strengths

These criteria are based on the principles of CHIME (Leamy et al, 2011) and are an attempt to translate that work to a higher level of analysis – namely the community and the city. This provides both a conceptual framework for recovery cities and a testable model that can be measured both at the initiation of the process and to measure growth and change in each of these component parts.

The concept of inclusive cities will also be beneficial for people dealing with the dual process of recovery and desistance. Similar to recovery theories, desistance acknowledges the importance of societal responses, next to individual/agency and social factors. Fairly recently, some desistance researchers have made distinctions between phases in the desistance process (Weaver, 2016). In this regard, Maruna and Farrall (2004) distinguished between 'primary' desistance, defined as an offence free period, focusing on a change in offending behaviour and 'secondary desistance', entailing the successful orientation towards a (permanent) offence free life, including developing a narrative to construct a new identity as a non-offender. Theories on desistance and recovery share common grounds: they are both transformational processes, which are not linear but dynamic, gradual and subject to relapse, and similar internal and external components seem to influence both processes of change.

These are the starting points for the development of a model that aims to create sustainable connections and networks in each city that will benefit those with addiction and offending histories by creating pathways to hope and reintegration and will create sustainable partnerships within the city. In the language of recovery capital (Best and Laudet, 2010), this generates community capital, a resource beyond the individual and that will benefit the whole community. Thus, the process is generative and can grow to meet the needs of each city. As our Life in Recovery study in the UK suggests (Best et al, 2015a), people in long-term recovery are highly likely (80% of those with more than five years) to be active contributors to their own community in the form of volunteering and participation in community groups and activities. Why does this happen? At least in part it happens because of the connections people make during the recovery process (Best, 2014) and the resulting positive social capital they can engage in. And this is something that grows over time.

However, engaging in activities such as ABCD has a generative effect in its own right as outlined in Chapter 6 on the Community Connectors project in Sheffield. In essence, as we learned in the early Australian projects (Chapter 2), the process of developing a network of connectors is in itself developmental and creates new opportunities and pathways. These groups represent the foundations for establishing bonds but also generate links and bridges (Putnam, 2000) that can be utilised and sustained to support the process of growth and evolution. The aim of the recovery cities model is to build exactly these kinds of coalitions that can generate hope and can build partnerships to support individual pathways and to build community cohesion and active participation in community activities.

The values underpinning this work are around creating a 'therapeutic landscape'(Wilton and DeVerteuil, 2006) that supports reintegration and celebrates success, for people with alcohol and drug problems, offending histories but ultimately for all excluded and marginalised groups in Doncaster. This aspiration is predicated on the idea that mobilisation of community resources is sustainable and can be processed through both a top-down and a bottom-up model of active engagement and through the contagion of hope. This should act as a form of both prevention and recovery support as communities become more receptive and connected, and so the benefits go beyond the recovery population to have a positive effect on the wellbeing of communities and all who live in them.

Summary and overview

This chapter has summarised two programmes of work in neighbouring cities that have had the same shared objective of celebrating the successes of recovery and creating a visible landscape of recovery with the aim of improving community life and reducing stigmatisation and social exclusion, through a process of creating a contagion of hope via community connections. The vision for both cities is based on the idea of capital as something that grows between people for the benefit of each of them (the helper gains as much as the person that is helped), but with a residual benefit at a collective level.

In Sheffield, SARRG provided a forum for bringing together professionals, policy makers, academics and peers to support and celebrate recovery activities. The group met monthly to prepare for quarterly events that generated bonding and bridging social capital and that were highly visible to challenge negative public perceptions and to build meaningful bridges into the recovery resources available across the city (which are discussed in Chapter 6). There was a clear strategy here that represented a 'top-down' strategic vision for building a visible recovery community linked to practice and evidence, but this evolved over time as local assets and local opportunities arose. The basic structure of quarterly events provided the framework and the springboard for this activity but it was the marriage of strategic vision and partnership combined with 'bottom-up' engagement and activities in a range of local communities that made the model successful and sustainable. SARRG had no formal membership model and both organisations and people drifted in and out of involvement but that is an inevitable part of the process of growing organic recovery partnerships and resources. The work in Sheffield continues to be inspired by committed people who support each other and who actively champion positive change in the city, and it is the hope that things like the PhD studentship will lead to sustainable recovery pathways and networks in Sheffield.

In Doncaster, there was a similar inspiration that derived from the incredible efforts of treatment services and local recovery communities, who had previously celebrated recovery through the Recovery Games annual event and through a series of conferences and training events. The Recovery College is an incredibly exciting development that is based on the same principle of bringing together organisations with shared values and philosophies in order to build bonds and links that create the opportunity not only for learning but also for capacity building and community building, particularly in the area of coalitions between professionals and peers. This has provided the foundation for the idea that Doncaster can be championed as a recovery city and that we can use recovery as a mechanism for building social justice and building stronger, fairer and better connected communities for all citizens.

Further, it is worth noting that the recovery cities model is taking off not only in Doncaster but also in Ghent (led by Dr Charlotte Colman) and in Gothenburg (led by Linda Nilsson and Mulka Nisic), and there are a number of other candidate cities emerging to support this process and growth.

Key lessons

- In keeping with the model proposed by Kelly and White (2011), recovery-oriented systems require a strategic vision with policy and practice engagement that creates a platform for community and peer participation and empowerment.
- A strengths-based model at a city level has to champion success and celebrate the achievements of recovery and desistance as part of a project of challenging stigma and exclusion.
- This is based on ideas of social justice and natural justice that extend beyond offending and substance use populations and that aim to promote community engagement and participation, with an ultimate goal of greater community connections leading to more effective social inclusion and greater access to community resources for marginalised populations.
- Underlying these ideas are the principles of personal and social capital growing and emerging to create new types of capital at a community level that are accessible and available to those in need. These are the foundations for a therapeutic landscape for recovery in which places are transformed in a way that promotes inclusion and wellbeing.
- There cannot be a fixed model for how this is done as community engagement is an evolving process where strengths will emerge through local assets and through unpredicted new networks, partnerships and synergies.
- In both Doncaster and Sheffield, the key success drivers have been the underlying qualities of connections, hope, and a shared and positive sense of identity, providing people with meaning and direction, and offering a sense of empowerment.
- This is contagious and generates both individual wellbeing and collective hope, and the idea of recovery cities is gathering momentum as a means of inspiring and promoting recovery and inclusion at a civic level.

6

Developing an initiative to support community connections

In this chapter I will review one of the projects that fell out of the SARRG partnership, involving multiple agencies applying for, and then receiving, research and development funding from a prestigious UK funder, the Health Foundation. The aim of the project was to recruit and train professional staff and people in long-term recovery, support them to become community connectors and then to apply that training to working with people new to recovery to engage with positive community assets. The chapter will review the process of bringing this project to life and the findings from the project, including some learnings about things that could have been done differently. However, the main conclusion is around the legacy and the sustainability of this project in Sheffield and also about its potential replication in other settings. However, prior to this, the initial section of the chapter will review some of the evidence around recovery champions and peers, and the role of the community connector.

Recovery pathways and recovery champions

As Best et al (2015c: 28) have argued in a review of the recovery evidence for the Scottish Government:

> Peer-based recovery support services can also play a significant role in eliminating or minimising the obstacles to treatment participation and recovery initiation via motivational priming, education about treatment

> and recovery, logistical support (e.g. transportation, child care, recovery-conducive housing), assistance in reconstructing social relationships, mobilising family support and countering any efforts to sabotage recovery initiation, and coaching to counter social stigma related to treatment participation.

The review goes on to point out that peer community based activity takes three primary forms:

1. Outreach is the extension of professional addiction treatment services into the life of the community, including supporting clients within their natural environments following the completion of primary treatment. Outreach strategies include community education efforts, early case identification and engagement via formal outreach, linking local harm reduction and recovery support resources, delivering services in non-traditional service sites, and enhancing the community visibility of people in long-term recovery.
2. In-reach is the inclusion of indigenous community resources within professionally directed addiction treatment. In-reach strategies include engaging each person's family and social network in the treatment process; establishing strong linkages between indigenous recovery support groups and addiction treatment institutions; and utilising consumer councils, alumni associations and volunteer programmes to saturate the treatment milieu with people representing diverse styles of long-term recovery. This is one mechanism for overcoming a 'silo' model where professional treatments exist in a separate and unconnected realm to the recovery activities in communities and in voluntary organisations.
3. Recovery community building encompasses activities that nurture the development of cultural institutions in which persons recovering from severe alcohol and other drugs (AOD) problems can find relationships that are recovery supportive, natural (reciprocal), accessible at times of greatest need (such as nights and weekends) and potentially enduring. Recovery community building activities include cultivating

> local recovery community (advocacy) organisations and peer-based recovery support groups, promoting the development of local peer-based recovery support services/institutions focusing on such areas as recovery-focused housing, education, employment and leisure. (White, 2009)

There is a clear link between peer-based recovery support services, as outlined in White's monograph, and community engagement and activity with the assumption being that peer champions or advocates are already established and embedded in a range of community resources and activities. The Home Office (2010) affords a critical role to the group of people they refer to as 'recovery champions' as people with some kind of relevant lived experience who are willing to discard anonymity and to actively engage with people in active use and in early recovery to support their recovery pathways and recovery journeys. The UK strategy was heavily criticised for failing to specify what credentials, training and support such individuals would need, and what the career pathways would be for this group. There was also no goals or objectives set by the Home Office (2010) around the number or retention of recovery champions. While any reader who has got this far in the book will be aware of the central role afforded to peers and their role in the contagion of hope and recovery spread, this does not mean that this group does not need considerable support and guidance in their roles and a clear sense of direction.

It is important to bear in mind that caveat when considering the development of peer-based services, although the involvement of peers at all levels and in all roles is consistent with the social contagion model that is central to this book. There is a strong supportive evidence base for peer-delivered interventions, with Humphreys and Lembke (2013) concluding that, along with mutual aid and recovery housing, peer-delivered recovery interventions are the most strongly-supported forms of intervention in terms of evidence base. They reported a randomised study that compares an entirely professionally-led treatment programme with one with 50% less staff but higher expectations of patient self-management, involvement and mutual support (Galanter et al, 1987). This study showed no difference in substance use outcomes by programme, as well as superior social adjustment among patients who participated in the peer-led programme. While there is limited trial evidence (although this study is by no means the only one), there is a strong body of cohort research that shown the benefits of peer intervention – and this is a two-way street. Not only does the participant attain gains that are often equivalent or superior to professionally delivered interventions, there is also the 'helper principle'. Akin to the 12th step of AA, this means that those who are helpers also benefit from the interaction and the positive sense of self and attainment and efficacy that derives from participation. The helper principle was first described by Riessman (1965) as indicating that those in a helping role receive many benefits, perhaps more than the recipient of help. The helper principle is central to the dynamic role of recovery spread in communities as it implies mutual gain and collective benefit – resulting in a growth of social and recovery capital.

The appeal of this model is entirely consistent with both a social capital and a social contagion model. As Moos (2007) has argued, two of the key principles for supporting recovery are social learning and social control, based on the idea that exposure to successful examples of recovery affords opportunities for learning and that this learning helps to build relationships that bind individuals into the values, norms and principles of recovery. It is also consistent with a social contagion idea that recovery spreads through communities in a manner similar to the contagion of a virus. Thus, the recovery capital of both parties can grow in a peer-based recovery model resulting in a greater pool and reserve of community capital, as a sort of ripple effect throughout not only the recovery but also the wider community.

This model originates in the work on the Framingham Heart Study undertaken by Christakis and Fowler and summarised in the book *Connected* (Christakis and Fowler, 2009). Based on a longitudinal study of disease spread in a US town, the authors derived four basic principles for the dissemination of not only illness but a range of socially mediated behaviours:

1. *We shape our networks and our network shapes us.* We become like the people we spend time with. 'Transivity' (i.e. the

amount of connections we have) affects the quality of our lives.

2. *Our friends affect us.* We often copy our friends, and critically for the work on desistance and recovery, our friends give us permission (and safety) to do things.
3. *Our friends' friends' friends affect us.* We are influenced by what our friends do – but also by our friends' friends – and surprisingly by our friends' friends' friends. Likewise what we do ripples out through three levels of friends before it loses its energy and impact. This is why not only bonding capital but also bridging capital is important to the model of social contagion of recovery and hope.
4. *Networks have a life of their own.* No one controls or owns the network. It is complex, dynamic and constantly evolving. This is similar to how a flock of geese has no leader but it self organises. It has no central control point but rather a 'shared intelligence'.

The basis for these findings is a series of assessments done every three to five years with members of the adult population of Framingham. The study ran for around 20 years with adults in Framingham completing a medical, giving a blood sample and completing a research interview. The key part of the research interview is that it assessed social connections based on who you know. This allowed the research team to complete a series of social network analyses locating individuals within networks – and it was on the basis of these networks that the demonstrated behaviours spread. While the dissemination of heart disease can be explained in simple biological spread, for other behaviours, it is less obvious what the mechanism of change is. One example of this is obesity:

- A person's odds of becoming obese increased by 57% if they had a friend who became obese, with a lower risk rate for friends of friends, lower again at three degrees of separation.
- No discernible effect at further levels of remove.

Similarly, smoking cessation by a spouse decreased a person's chances of smoking by 67%, while smoking cessation by a friend decreased the chances by 36%. The average risk of smoking at one degree of separation (that is, smoking by a friend) was 61% higher, 29% higher at two degrees of separation and 11% higher at three degrees of separation.

The beauty of the design is that multiple time points means that the predictions made on the basis of one time point are actually tested at the next wave of data collection, and so changes in behaviours of one person at the baseline can be used to predict changes in the behaviours of the members of their networks at follow-up points. There are two key points that have emerged from this method:

1. If person A names person B as a friend at time 1, then person B's behaviour will influence person A more than the other way around (the authors referred to this as the relationship between the principal and the alter).
2. Geographic distance makes no difference: If you do not know your next door neighbour, then physical proximity alone will not influence behaviour. Likewise, close friends with whom you have regular contact will influence your behaviour irrespective of how close physically they live. This is part of the reason why online communities can be so powerful and so effective in supporting recovery pathways.

In a follow-up paper about binge drinking, Rosenquist et al (2010) found that, on the basis of 12,067 people from whom data were collected every 2–4 years:

- Principals are 50% more likely to drink heavily if a person they are directly connected to drinks heavily; 36% more likely at two degrees of separation; 15% at three degrees of separation.
- People are 29% more likely to abstain if someone they are directly connected to abstains. This effect is 21% at two degrees of separation; 5% at three degrees of separation.

It is apparent that this is a bi-directional effect – in other words, there is a constant tension around behaviours regarding which will dominate based on their perceived attractiveness, and their capacity to spread through networks. This means that there are competing processes around the contagion of smoking and around the contagion of smoking cessation. What will predominate will be determined by group behaviours and norms embedded in broader cultural values and behaviours. In the language of Christakis and Fowler (2010) what is spread is the contagion and how it spreads is through processes of connection. There is a third theme called 'homophily', which is based on the premise that people are connected to those who are similar to them in terms of values and attitudes. This relates closely to social identity ideas of group membership where shared values and beliefs are a core part of being a member of a group with changes in the values or behaviour of a central and valued member of the group (for example, switching from caffeinated to decaffeinated coffee) likely to spread through the group.

The underlying model for community connections is around two principles – the importance of peers, and the nature of group membership and the idea of social identity. As outlined, there is good evidence for the importance of peers in delivering and supporting recovery wellbeing (Humphreys and Lembke, 2013). Peers will generally afford homophily to a greater extent than professionals and they will be seen as more accessible and more available. Additionally, they will also provide the role modelling and social learning (Moos, 2007) that is to be the focal point for the contagion (through living and modelling the desired behaviours to be disseminated) and they will act as the connections to groups that model pro-social behaviour. Crucially, they will also be members of the same recovery groups and communities and so be perceived as part of 'us' by their recovery peers and, therefore, their behaviour and beliefs will be more influential.

The impact of groups on identity

A study of 141 cocaine-dependent individuals by Zywiak and colleagues (2009) found that patients who had better treatment outcomes typically had larger social networks, more frequent contact with their social network, and an increase over time in the proportion of people in their social network who did not use any substances, including alcohol. In other words, among people with problems relating to cocaine use, those with the best outcomes were more socially connected, particularly with social groups whose norms were not supportive of continued substance use. Similarly, Litt et al (2007, 2009) reported on a randomised controlled trial involving people who completed residential detoxification from alcohol and were then randomly allocated to either standard aftercare or to a 'network support' intervention that involved developing a relationship with at least one non-drinking peer. Compared to standard aftercare, those who added at least one non-drinking member to their social network showed a 27% increase at 12 months post-treatment in the likelihood of treatment success (defined as being without alcohol 90% of the time). It is not surprising that most of those in the network support condition were recruited from 12-step mutual aid groups and were peers who were giving back as part of their own recovery pathway and journey.

This chimes with my own first recovery study (Best et al, 2008) where, using a very basic survey research method and recruiting from recovery meetings, we found that while there were a diverse range of reasons for how people achieved abstinence, sustaining recovery was largely due to both moving away from using networks and into sober and recovery networks. While the strongest predictor of stopping was a combination of being tired of the lifestyle and some trigger event (losing a job, a relationship ending, being arrested or a health crisis), sustaining recovery was generally reported to be a social experience, and engaging in positive and pro-social groups. Over the course of the next ten years, my work has largely focused on what such changes mean and involve. The studies have consistently shown the importance of social groups and the resulting sense of identity and belonging.

This fits into a social identity model of change that is outlined in our 2016 paper (Best et al, 2016). Social identity theory proposes that, in a range of social contexts, people's sense of self is derived from their membership of various social groups. The resulting social identities serve to structure (and restructure) a person's perception and behaviour — their values, norms and goals; their orientations, relationships and interactions; what they think, what they do, and what they want to achieve (Tajfel and Turner, 1979; Haslam, 2014). The core point of the model is that groups not only provide a sense of belonging, purpose and support (Cruwys et al, 2014; Dingle et al, 2012; Haslam and Reicher, 2006; Jetten et al, 2012b), but also provide a basis for influencing others (Turner, 1991). Thus, social capital is about much more than a group of people to go for dinner with or talk to about your problems or even about borrowing a kettle or a van from. It is about the health conferring sense of benefit and belonging that stems from belonging to groups that support wellbeing and provide an affirmation of your views and beliefs, and a source of understanding and making sense of many of the challenges that you face.

While there has long been a recognition that a key part of recovery is a change of identity (Biernacki, 1986; McIntosh and McKeganey, 2000), the focus has largely been on personal rather than social identity – the latter referring to the identity resources that people draw from the groups they are a member of. The assumption was that people who had experienced addictions (and extensive involvement in criminal justice settings) had both been labelled in a negative way and had internalised a part of that internalisation – what McIntosh and McKeganey referred to as a 'spoilt identity' that had to be 'restored' as part of a recovery process. The transition to a social model of identity change founds this restoration in group membership, as previously reported in the discussion of Jobs, Friends and Houses and in particular the research presented about the analysis of the JFH Facebook page posts.

In collaboration with colleagues from Melbourne and Brisbane, we outlined the SIMOR (Best et al, 2016). This drew heavily on social identity theory and used AA as an example of how group membership can result in changes in identity through the internalisation of the values and norms of new groups the person belongs to. 12-step groups can attract and retain people into the values and principles of the Fellowship through a very strong social identification process that changes not only social networks (and resulting social capital) but values and beliefs around drinking but extending into wider life values and activities. This is what

Jetten et al (2012b) had referred to as 'The Social Cure', in which membership of positively valued groups results in positive changes in not only self-concept but also in wellbeing. The argument here is that recovery is a process in which

> Their identification with a recovery group will shape their understanding of substance-related events (e.g. an offer to go to the pub with friends) and their response to it (rejection on the grounds that it would put their recovery at risk). In sum, group memberships exert influence on individuals through the transmission of social norms which are internalised, and shape subsequent attitudes and behaviour. (Best et al, 2016: 9)

This means that the individual comes to interpret new situations according to the values of the group if those values fit the context (that is, they are about alcohol or drugs) and are readily accessible to their minds. Thus, belonging to pro-social groups that are perceived to be attractive, and that the individual values being a member of, makes the values and beliefs of that group more prominent and more likely to be deployed when faced with a high risk situation. The individual will not want to engage in activities that will risk the valued group membership (for example, by drinking thus contravening the rules of the recovery group). More importantly, however, the temptation to go to the pub will be diminished by recognising this as a risk of drinking – such as in the AA mantra that 'you don't go to the barbers if you don't expect to get a haircut'. The more actively the individual is embedded in the recovery group the more salient and accessible the values of the group are and the more the individual has to lose by being excluded from the group.

However, this transition process is not enough in itself and it is not possible to assume that people will always have the strength of will nor even the opportunity to make the transition to pro-social or recovery groups. The remainder of this chapter looks at how people can be encouraged to move from using to recovery groups and what supports they are likely to need to initiate and sustain this process. The method described below is based on an organisational partnership and external funding that supported a city-wide initiative to develop a cohort of community connectors that were trained and supported to provide guidance and direction to people early in their recovery journeys.

The foundations for community connections in Sheffield

The project described here builds on the partnerships and connections outlined in Chapter 5, and in particular the coordination of local recovery activities and endeavours brought together through SARRG. Through a number of community activities, the City Council (in the form of the Drug and Alcohol Commissioning Team), the local NHS Trust (SHSC), SASS and Sheffield Hallam University agreed to partner in making a funding proposal to the Health Foundation to develop a project on community connections in the city. The project was built on a partnership and trusting relationships established as a part of the work described in Chapter 5.

In March 2015, an application was made to the Innovating for Improvement funding round from the Health Foundation, competing against proposals across the fields of health and social care. The title of the proposal was 'Building local pathways to community capital, social capital and connectedness to improve wellbeing outcomes: Building professional networks in local communities'. The project used alcohol and drug problems as a pilot to this model and began by improving local frontline professionals' capacity to support community engagement through active engagement with and participation in local communities. By doing so, the aim was to establish a group of 'community connectors' (professionals and community members) to act as the bridges to existing resources in the community, and to build partnerships with existing community groups and activities for those service users accessing drug and alcohol facilities in Sheffield. The Health Foundation project drew on many of the same values and principles as the recovery cities work described in Chapter 5.

The project, REC-CONNECT, had five phases:

1. To train alcohol and drug workers in the principles of assertive linkage (defined as professional and peer support to enable vulnerable individuals to engage effectively and to integrate with positive and pro-social groups in the community) into communities and to build links with positive social groups. Alongside raising workers' awareness of local recovery resources, by providing results from a local community asset mapping exercise, this will result in a process mapping of community assets and individuals who will be identified as potential candidates for the community connectors group, who will then be trained to link in to community assets.
2. To provide a community connector recruitment, training and support programme, based on the assertive linkage training model to be delivered to this mixed professional, peer and community group of community connectors. Community connectors are respected and known members of local communities who are able to attract, engage and link vulnerable individuals with local community assets that they have knowledge of and access to.
3. The provision of ongoing support for the community connectors to engage with clients of the alcohol and drug services in Sheffield, assertively linking them into local resources and pro-social groups and activities, increasing their social and community capital resources, and supporting the connector group to deliver effective linkage.
4. To evaluate both the impact of the training provided and test if this model improves engagement in community groups and social capital in vulnerable populations, starting with a group in early recovery from alcohol and drug problems (does it improve wellbeing and reduce engagement in harmful behaviours?).
5. To disseminate findings to local and national stakeholders, discuss replicability in different health settings and with different service user cohorts, and the development of a tool kit for wider dissemination and the sharing of good practice.

Thus, the aims of the project were community engagement and community connections, developed in a model of co-production and with the aim of community enhancement and development. To translate this into the language of social and community capital, the aims of the project were:

- To build recovery capital in the group of clients new to recovery processes who see themselves as ready to move on to the next stage of their journey.
- To do this by providing social capital in the form of mentors/navigators who are further on in their recovery journeys and can role model successful recovery beliefs and practices.
- The navigators/connectors also act as bridges to new activities and to new social groups that can generate social capital and access to resources in the community, and they are provided with training and support to enhance this role.
- The navigators/connectors not only benefit from the 'helper principle' but also from developing new bridging and linking connections themselves, and through being a part of the connector group.

Moreover, there are two sustainable benefits that result:

1. Services and organisations across the city become better connected and more effectively integrated.
2. The process undertaken of mapping and linking into community assets in itself generates new community assets and resources – in other words, the process is generative.

The process of building community connections and connectors

There were a number of core phases in the project, as described opposite, that yielded the following outcomes.

Phase 1: Awareness raising

In the initial phase of the project, team members from each of the partner organisations attended events and meetings across the city to raise awareness of the project and to recruit our cohort of navigator/connectors.

Phase 2

As a consequence, three training sessions were held with a total of 52 participants, who were a combination of workers in specialist addiction services, peer volunteers, staff and students from Sheffield Hallam University and managers from the participating services. These training sessions covered the following core activities:

- explanations of the purpose of community connections;
- explanations of the evidence for assertive linkage;
- undertaking an ABCD activity that identified recovery supportive assets that each connector already had links into in the areas of sport and recreation, education and training, community engagement and mutual aid; and
- what the core characteristics were of those would be successful community connectors – both at an individual level and at a group level.

Phase 3: In-depth training: Workshops

Using the feedback from the information sessions, the research team subsequently designed workshops around ABCD and assertive linkage, delivering them to 41 workers and service users. Workshop participants completed ABCD maps and identified what they considered to be the ideal attributes of a community connector, thus co-designing the 'job description' for their role. We exceeded our recruitment and training targets in the other two stages of our project. We recruited and trained 21 community connectors (target = 15), with others requesting to join the scheme after the training concluded. We trained over 40 workers (target = 20), volunteers and peers in the techniques of assertive linkage and in particular how this community engagement could be used to enhance the choices and rights of the person in recovery.

This not only had the effect of providing us with a cohort of connectors for the next stage, it also created a much broader support base for the project across organisations and across grades of seniority and professions, an ideal example of both bridging capital and linking capital.

Evidence of the impact of the training programme comes from the evaluations received from participants. To summarise the findings from the pre-launch training sessions (n=63):

- broadly positive responses to the value of the training they had received, benefits to job and clients, and increased knowledge;
- concerns around time and resources to utilise the methods; and
- key areas of learning were strongly endorsed with all domains scoring 3.5 or higher on a 1–5 scale, with 1 reflecting lower value and 5 higher value; only 'will not work' scored below 2, suggesting a general belief in the implementation and application of the approach.

For the evaluation, we utilised a bespoke version of the Texas Christian University (TCU) Organizational Readiness for Change Workshop Evaluation form (WEVAL), chosen as it measures readiness to implement training in applied settings.

On scales ranging from 1–5, where higher scores represent stronger endorsement of that factor, the standard measures of how satisfied the participant was and how relevant the materials were are consistently positively endorsed. For a diverse group of connectors, it is key that the participants 'feel comfortable' in using the materials and that those materials will be useful in supporting their role as connectors. As important in this kind of model are perceived barriers to effective implementation and the general perception was that (with the exception of some concern about the time required) there were no significant barriers to implementation. Again using the same scaling of 1–5 with higher scores indicating greater levels of endorsement, there is little indication that resources, lack of training or lack of belief in the materials represent significant barriers to effective implementation.

Phase 4: Community asset mapping

The group of 21 connectors engaged in a series of workshops and events to identify community assets that people early in recovery could be linked into. The idea of having a mixture of professionals, volunteers and peers was that they would have access to different groups – they would not all be tapping into the same community capital. This is based on the idea that each person is likely to need a different configuration of groups and supports to match their needs, passions and interests but also that these needs will evolve over the course of the recovery journey. Nonetheless, the starting point for the asset mapping activities were in the standard group of four categories, as used in several of the other projects described in this volume:

- sports and recreation (including involvement in the arts);
- education, training and employment;
- volunteering and community engagement; and
- mutual aid and recovery groups.

Participants were asked to identify the standard three categories of assets – people, informal groups and associations, and formal organisations and institutions – but were asked only to include those that they had some form of personal contact and engagement with.

Through this process a total of 134 assets were identified in Sheffield and the surrounding areas that our connectors had some method of engagement with, and these are depicted in Figures 6.1 to 6.4.

As can be seen in Figure 6.1, these assets are diverse in terms of the range of activities and groups, reflecting the group of connectors who came up with the list. Thus, there is at least

Figure 6.1: Recreation and sport assets

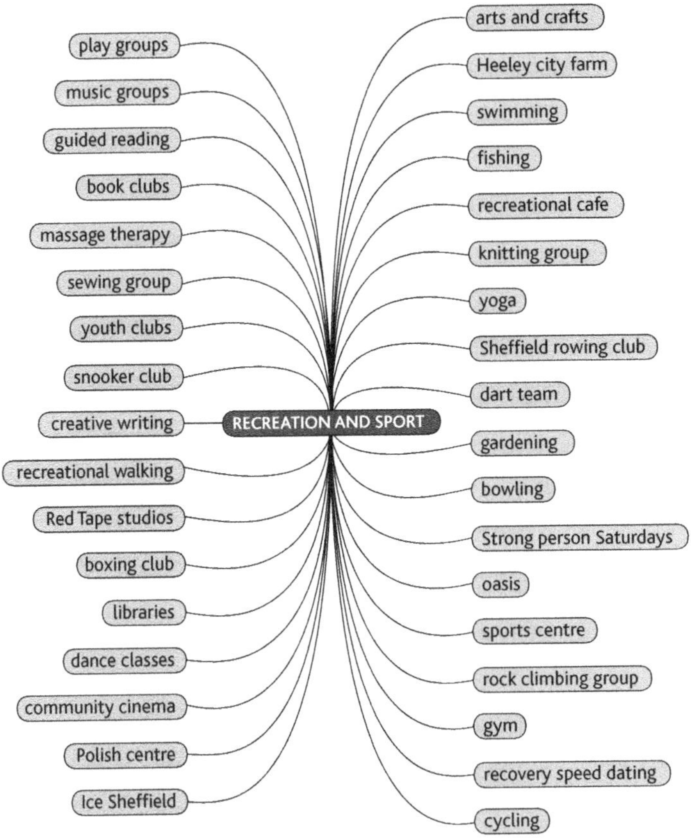

one group that is linked to a minority ethnic community (Polish), and things as diverse as libraries, community cinema and rock climbing. Although some of these groups are specifically targeted at people in recovery that is not stated in the depiction of the groups, although the navigators were aware of this distinction. Figure 6.2 outlines the mutual aid groups that were identified.

Mutual aid groups range from the main 12-step fellowship groups (CA, NA and so on) to more unusual groups such as Workaholics Anonymous and a local recovery café, as well as to local friends groups and individual community activities

Figure 6.2: Mutual aid groups assets

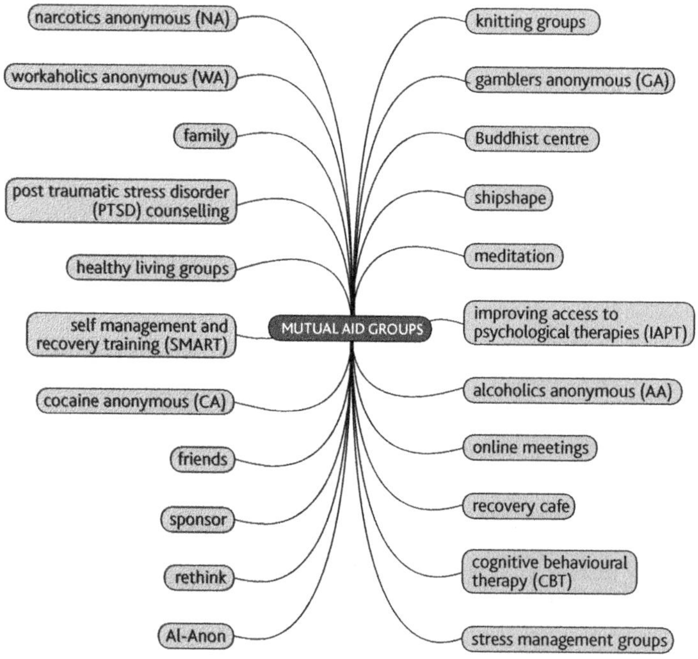

and groups. The point is to identify choice and none of the navigators/connectors knew all of the groups or activities that were identified. That is part of the aim of the activity – it generates new knowledge and new connections as well as building on what is already there so that the repertoires of all of the navigators grow. For all of those participating in the exercise, it is a generative exercise that links connectors to each other and augments their sense of engagement in and belonging to their communities. In Figure 6.3, the overview of peer and community assets is provided.

The assets identified in Figure 6.3 are incredibly diverse and range from those that would be expected in most communities, such as recovery support services and recovery community groups, to more diverse interests and activities that may be unique to one particular community. Again the assumption is not that every asset will be accessible by all clients (there are several women's only groups, for instance) but that every

Figure 6.3: Peer and community assets

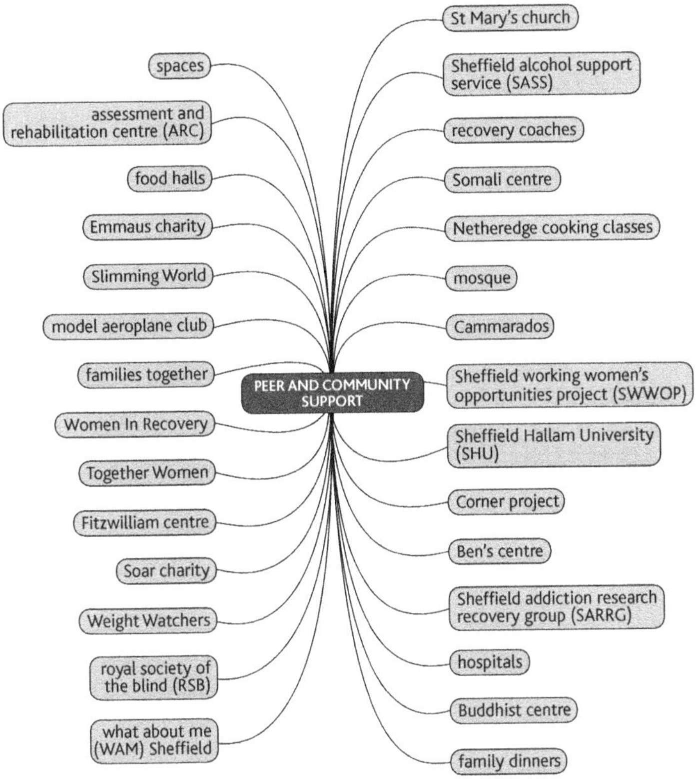

asset has a potential role to play in the recovery pathways for at least some people in early recovery, and that all may help to build the community capital of the recovery community at a collective level. There are also some religious organisations listed (church, mosque) and this has two implications; first, that they may have groups or activities that can help people in their recovery, and the second is that spiritual and religious involvement may be an important part of recovery for many people (White, 2009). In some settings, it may be appropriate to list them as a separate category of recovery resources and that can be determined by the preferences of the group. The final set of resources related to education and employment and are shown in Figure 6.4.

Figure 6.4: Educational and employment assets

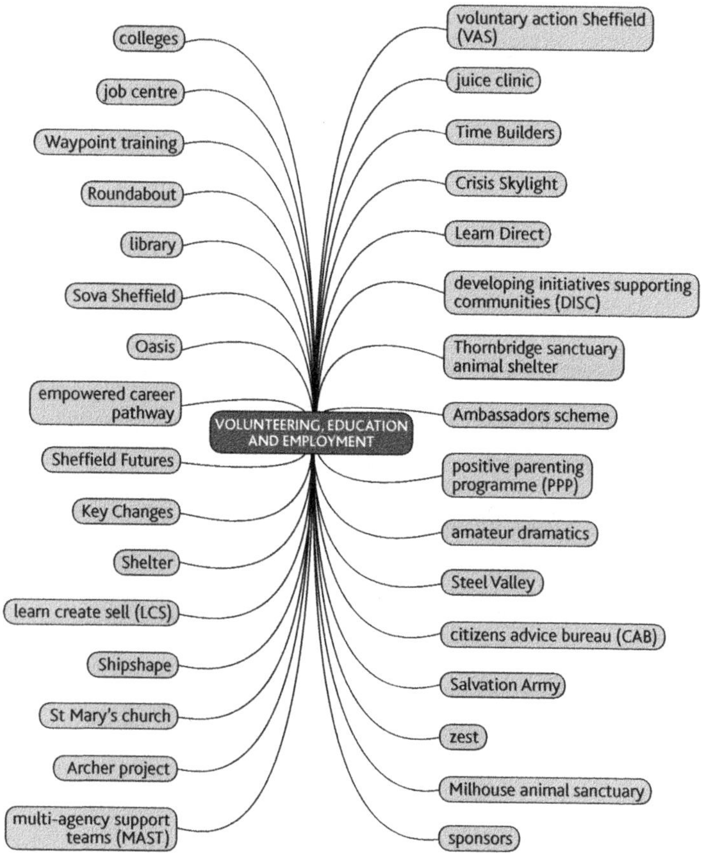

As in the categories already discussed, listed in Figure 6.4 are the more obvious resources such as the local colleges, training providers and the job centre, but also a remarkable diversity of other organisations who can help people get started with skill building including in the areas of parenting and animal welfare, proffering richness and diversity to recovery pathways and hopefully inspiring the imagination of both connectors and their clients. Again a number of spiritual organisations like churches and the Salvation Army are listed here as they can offer both volunteering opportunities and access to community resources and community capital.

For both desistance and recovery, having a meaningful occupation that provides money as well as a sense of pride and self-worth is an important predictor of recovery (for example, Cano et al, 2017) but also provides a psychological barrier to relapse and reoffending (this was referred to as behavioural economics by Moos, 2007), and as a form of informal social control (Laub and Sampson, 2003) that supports rehabilitation and reintegration by binding people back into conventional groups and activities. It is recognised that for many people with addiction histories there are barriers and challenges in attaining the desired forms of employment – including disrupted work histories and criminal records – and so the options listed in Figure 6.4 include some very early steps (volunteering and college courses) that will make people more ready and more attractive to the employment market.

Phase 5: Becoming a connector, and the connectors developing into an asset

While the group of 21 navigators/connectors recruited into the Sheffield Community Connectors project already had a diverse range of skills and assets, there were three further tasks that needed to be completed to prepare them for actively supporting people new to recovery in their journeys:

1. Ensuring that the list of assets identified were viable and that the links to them were positive and realistic for people to utilise. It is here that both a model of in-reach and outreach can be used depending on the group to help to consolidate and build a sustainable pathway and to ensure a positive reception for clients who choose to engage with that asset.
2. Identifying a set of rules and protocols to ensure that the connectors/navigators would be safe and operate within guidelines that were consistent and transparent. This also contributes to the sustainability of the model and helps to ensure that connectors and the groups they engage with are dealt with consistently and within agreed boundaries and parameters.

3. Working together to identify their own developmental and support needs and to make sure that this was a positive experience for participants. It is critical for the effectiveness of the approach that all the participants feel that they benefit from their participation. We were very clear with the connectors that their development and growth, of both the group as a new asset and the recovery community more collectively, were central objectives of the project.

There was no assumption that the connectors were all the same and indeed it was recognised that, as a coalition of professionals, peers, family members and volunteers from the community, they would be coming from very different places, and with very different resources and supports, and developmental needs. While the group did some work on what desirable characteristics for recovery navigators were – and came up with a list of skills and attributes like tenacity, energy, enthusiasm and good social and support skills – the focus was on their collective knowledge and skills rather than their individual attributes. The aim was to ensure that they received the support they needed collectively to enable them to work together and to support each other, and that they recognised that commitment to work with each other and to support each other.

Critically, they also worked with each other to identify and develop support mechanisms that shared some of the features of clinical supervision but much more strongly based on a peer model. This was not only designed to support the connectors but also to ensure consistency of process and to provide simple guidance and rules to those who got involved. It was always a priority of the project that its aims were to develop a cohort of connectors not only to have them operate as bridges to community resources but also to support and strengthen their wellbeing and, where appropriate, their own recovery resources and recovery needs. One of the main reasons why the cohort of connectors was intended to be a 'coalition' of recovery peers, professionals and other community members (such as family members) was to ensure that there was both a diversity of assets and skills that they could tap into but that they could come together to support each other and to create new connections and community resources.

Implementation and moving forward

The connector group met on a number of occasions to agree on processes such as communication and protocols for engaging and working with clients until they felt they were ready to actively recruit clients. The client group that had been specified for the project was a group of people who were in early recovery. By this time we had also extended the group of treatment providers to include a national community treatment provider (Addaction) and the local residential rehabilitation service (Phoenix Futures), as word of the project extended out into the community. Each agency was then contacted to encourage them to identify appropriate clients – who would either be preparing for a return to the community (in the case of residential services) or were making a transition to a recovery-oriented part of the treatment service. The inclusion criterion was that the client was new in their recovery journey and they were enthusiastic about improving their community engagement.

Phase 6: Active recruitment of clients new to recovery

It is important to note that although we were highly successful in training and engaging a highly charismatic, motivated and skilled group of navigators/connectors, we had more problems in engaging clients new to recovery to participate in the project. We recruited 17 clients from five agencies: SASS (n=5), Phoenix Futures (n=5), SHSC (n=4), Drink Wise Age Well (n=2) and Addaction (n=1). All were white British – 5 female and 12 male. There were particular problems with the NHS service where communication about the project to clients was extremely limited. We used the REC-CAP – a measure reported in Cano et al (2017) to measure recovery strengths and to examine barriers to recovery pathways.

Analysis of the data shows varying levels of wellbeing and recovery capital (indicated in means with low to high scale ranges):

- *Wellbeing:* There was a mean score of 61.5 on a 0–100 scale, where higher scores represent positive wellbeing. In comparison with other populations (such as clients of recovery residences, Cano et al, 2017), these are low scores and represent poor levels of wellbeing.
- *Personal recovery capital:* There was a mean score of 12.6 on a 0–25 scale. These are very poor scores and compared to both the means for the original recovery population tested on the Alcohol Recovery Community (ARC; Groshkova et al, 2012) and the US population from recovery residences (Cano et al, 2017) represents low levels of recovery capital.
- *Social recovery capital:* There was a mean score of 12.8 on a 0–25 scale. As with the personal capital scores, these are significantly lower than comparison groups, suggesting poor social networks and engagement, and this suggests significant work to be done in supporting their recovery pathways and journeys. This would suggest that although the sample was low, it did successfully recruit a cohort in significant need of improvements in their community engagement.

Groups and services engagement was reported as: eight of the participants engaged with 'other community recovery groups'; seven with peer support groups; five with online groups; and one with 12-step groups. In contrast, eight were receiving support from drug treatment services; 12 were receiving support from alcohol treatment services, and 15 were receiving primary healthcare services at the time of the baseline interview. What this suggests is that there was much greater involvement with acute care services than with recovery groups and services, and one of the core aims of the underlying recovery model is to help people transition to less professionally driven and more peer and community focused activities and groups.

We were unable to secure follow-up REC-CAP data for all recruits, because of logistical challenges around retaining clients in the study, and running out of time with regards funding. However, case studies from several clients and their reports revealed significant change and strongly endorsed the intervention. Clients reported a positive impact on their social wellbeing and recovery. For some, it provided an opportunity to try new things and meet new people, which before working with their community connector had been difficult. From a social capital perspective, there was evidence of gains in both bonding capital (within the connectors group) and bridging capital (improved networks and engagement with a wider range of communities), and some of these bridges are sustainable beyond the life of the project.

Case studies and their implications

The following three case studies, which illustrate the benefits of the project, are drawn from the final report submitted by the team to the Health Foundation. The names of both participants have been changed to protect their identities.

Case 1

Female, aged 27

First seen: 03/04/17

Susan walked into local service the ARC without an appointment. She had previously had support through the SHSC treatment service when she had issues with other substances, but now felt she was compensating with alcohol and had started to lose control of her drinking.

At first she did not show much motivation to make any changes to her alcohol use but after reviewing her recovery capital with an ARC Support Worker, it came to light that she really struggled during the evening, when a lot of services were closed. The ARC Worker suggested that she access some support groups in the evening, which is when she had the most trouble with urges and worries. Susan was very anxious about going to a meeting on her own, especially one she had never been to before and when offered a subscription to online support group Soberistas as an alternative, she did not feel comfortable enough with computers to get any benefit. This is when the worker thought our REC-CONNECT project might work.

The community connector based with the ARC team sat down and went through the REC-CAP, identifying what type of meeting would be most helpful for her to attend. The connector already had links in this area so was able to initiate a meeting with a female member of AA who the connector trusted and made sure that Susan would feel welcome.

Susan met the AA member, who has now become her sponsor and is taking her through a programme of recovery in an environment that Susan feels is friendly and safe. She continues to maintain her recovery and she can't quite believe the changes she has made to her life and continues to make in her recovery.

Case 2

Male, aged 38

First Seen: 17/03/17

John was struggling to keep his house tidy but was spending long periods of time at home on his own. He described the isolation and unpleasant environment as significant factors to his drinking; using alcohol as a way to help reduce his anxiety and help him socialise. He felt that finding some form of hobby that would get him out of the house and meeting people in a non-drinking environment would help him to reduce his drinking. He was particularly interested in walking.

The community connector helped John to make contact with a local walking group in Sheffield. However, John was not able to make the scheduled group walks but has maintained an interest and contact with the group leader. In the meantime, the community connector linked John into a local recovery upcycling activity called Rags to Riches that refurbishes furniture and household items. This has been perfect for John as there is a focus to the activity but also the opportunity to socialise in a less pressured way. He has reduced his alcohol use by half and appears to be less nervous around others. He has also used his new-found enthusiasm for recycling to tackle his own home.

What both case studies demonstrate is the importance of both relationships between the clients and the connectors and the diversity of community resources that the connectors were able to link the clients into. What the first case study also demonstrates is the impact that both the relationship and the connection can have on personal capital. In other words, the social capital afforded by the link to the navigator builds recovery resources in its own right as well as the benefits that are derived through the process of connection. In the case of Susan, this is about building confidence and a sense of wellbeing.

In the third case study, there is a very clear impact on wellbeing and quality of life.

Case 3

Female, aged 55

REC-CAP baseline date: 29/03/17

Charlotte suffered serious physical limitations as a result of her misuse of alcohol, and these are ongoing. She was hospitalised for seven weeks a few years ago and has not used alcohol since. However, she struggled because of her physical limitations. She uses a wheelchair or standing frame to get around, and has been essentially home-bound, resulting in feelings of social isolation. She was approached by a worker from Drink Wise Age Well (DWAW) about visiting their programme, and a staff member from DWAW picked her up and took her to an initial meeting where she was introduced to her community connector. She was unconvinced about completing the REC-CAP instrument initially, but then began getting involved with activities, and a recovery group, and by the time she completed her follow-up, she was feeling better and much more enthusiastic.

Charlotte said she 'feels better,' enjoys the 'different atmosphere' of her recovery group, who she described as 'like family'. She has a loving, caring son but needed connections. She attends mutual aid group meetings and does team work – putting together puzzles, making jewellery, candles and other crafts. Even with her physical limitations, she went on a group visit to an aquarium and was booked to visit a safari park the day after our talk but had to cancel due to her dog being seriously ill. She goes to DWAW fortnightly and said she thinks she could pack a bag and live there. With a hearty laugh, Charlotte said, "when I go down there [DWAW], I just let loose!"

This is the key to the dynamic process that is at the heart of the connections model. For people who lack social capital (pro-social networks and the resulting activities), at least in part as a result of a lack of personal capital (self-confidence, self-efficacy and communication skills), the connections model attempts to kick-start a process of change. With Charlotte, the initial positive link with the connector generated enough social capital that she was able to build the trust and the belief to actively engage in at first one group activity, and then a number of them, that result in a form of social cure to the extent that she now has a wider network of support and a range of activities and networks with whom she feels safe and comfortable.

All three of the case studies are based on the same premise – that a good connector can make a personal contact with the client, and build both trust and enthusiasm in their relationship as the foundation for effective connection. On this basis, the person can be persuaded (based on the trust generated) to venture out to do things that they would not previously have considered – but not just anything, things that match with their interests and passions. This is the purpose of the model – to inspire people through relational means to build a 'virtuous circle' of personal, social and community capital that will enable them to develop and grow. They engage in new activities, so they meet new people and have the possibility of developing new social networks and identities and forming their own bridges to community assets.

Although the numbers who were effectively engaged and followed up were too low for systematic assessment of changes in wellbeing, the overall impact of the project was positive, with a twin process of cyclical and reciprocal growth.

Virtuous circle 1: Client growth and recovery – as outlined in the three case studies, there is clear evidence that stimulating social capital can generate initially community capital (through active engagement with external assets) and then personal capital (through the impact on wellbeing, belonging and connectedness that constitutes virtuous circle 1).

Virtuous circle 2: There is a second type of benefit that derives from the project – at the centre of this circle are the clients who benefit through the process of connections (through bonding, bridging and linking capital). At the second level, there is a growing partnership between peer volunteers and professionals who acted as connectors/navigators in the project. They also developed new sets of connections and alliances not only to allow them to support the clients in the project but also to improve their own bridging and linking social capital. Finally, at the third level, the project led to increased trust and cooperation between the participating organisations, who worked more closely together. As at the client level, there is a relationship between these three layers and the growth in one prompts and promotes growth in the other two. The argument to be advanced here is that this creates a therapeutic landscape for change. The argument that will be developed in the next section is that this emerges from a shared ownership or co-production of community assets. Furthermore, the two levels described here are linked dynamically such that growth in organisations increases the likelihood of growth for their clients.

Co-producing recovery systems

In outlining the key principles of a recovery-oriented system of care, Sheedy and Whitter (2009) are clear that there needs to be a transition from an expert-patient model to a partnership approach and that the locus of change is the community not the clinic or hospital. Imperative to a co-production approach is the blurring of boundaries between the user and the professional

(Nutbrown et al, 2015); Pestoff and colleagues (2010) outline three key motivations for people willing to be involved in co-production: self-interest, civic obligation, and belonging to a co-producing social group. This model is ideally suited to a recovery approach where ownership is not only shared, but the sharing of ownership is an act of both trust and empowerment, that affords dignity and respect to people who, through various processes of stigmatisation and exclusion, will often have been denied this in the past. While peer-based approaches to both drug and alcohol treatment have become an expected part of more formal, medically-driven treatment pathways, this has not always been within a framework of active engagement and empowerment. And crucially, it has not always involved the sharing of either knowledge or power.

What made the REC-CONNECT programme relevant to co-production practice is the bringing together of professional and recovery peers to jointly train in assertive linkage and ABCD mapping, supporting and growing a 'mixed' group of community connectors and assessing their impact on wellbeing of the target population. Once the basic principles of each approach were explained and the theory and rationale described, key decisions about process and implementation were left to the group to shape. In other words, what is unique about this model and separates it from prior ABCD initiatives is that it has the goal of building community engagement in all participants (both professional and service user), with an anticipated ripple effect out through communities. From the outset the aim was to go beyond the basic research model to incorporate a 'legacy' approach that involved the empowerment of individual participants but every bit as important was the idea that the group of connector navigators had a role to play in developing and building their own roles and activities, and their place in the local community, and that the whole process would enrich the community and make it more engaging and inclusive.

This was possible because the project had co-production at its core in each stage of roll-out, and this was based on a coalition approach: from the 21 community connectors who were ultimately recruited, seven were NHS staff, seven were voluntary sector staff and seven were people in recovery (the recovery status of staff members was not investigated). There was very little evidence of stigma or exclusion from professional to service user within the group and the coalescence of the group and the recognition of the diversity of skills within the group was an important part of the process of establishing group norms and values.

Valuable feedback from participants included the success of the project in connecting previously siloed agencies and organisations. The relationships formed or enhanced within the project team and the lowering of the separation between researcher, professional and peer-driven services is a project success that will be key for sustainability. What the project has done is create a partnership for co-production that involves statutory organisation and NGOs, with a local university at a strategic level and engaged a range of individuals who are both professionals and volunteers to work together to generate and link to community resources.

There were limitations to the success of the co-production approach – in the end the project finance sat with the participating organisations and the academic outputs were largely driven and guided by the university, although a number of the connector navigators did take part in presentations and the dissemination of the impact of the work. And it is this group who are ultimately responsible for ensuring that legacy of the time-limited funding is meaningfully applied. The project did not view participants as a 'vulnerable' or excluded group and part of a strengths-based model is the aim of inclusion and participation at all levels.

Overview and discussion

The aim of co-production is empowerment and enrichment and can be translated into the language of capital in the form of social and community capital growth. What the project has been able to demonstrate is the richness and diversity of the assets that are available in the Sheffield area, but more importantly that are accessible to and can be engaged with by a group of people either working in drug and alcohol services or who are graduates and volunteers at those services. So the project has successfully answered two questions – first, that yes there are resources available in the community and, second, yes there are bridges through a small group of connectors to access those services. In contrast to the experiences with the family members of prisoners, the connector navigator groups had strong existing networks and access to community capital.

The project occurred in one city, Sheffield, where there is already a well-established recovery community and it is possible that some of the positive experiences here may be less easy to replicate in other locations where such a community does not already exist. However, it is also important to note that because this was a demonstration project, all of the assets were accessed over a short period of time – not much more than one month – and that in practice there would be an ongoing process of recruitment of connectors and navigators and a continuous effort at building bridges to new community resources while strengthening the bridges to existing resources.

It is also important to acknowledge and identify that one of the key legacy elements of the project is the creation of the cohort of navigator connectors as a coherent and integrated group moving forwards. As has been emphasised previously, the connectors model is not simply about products, it is also about process. Building a coherent network of connectors who come to identify with the group and take pride and a positive sense of identity from their membership is an important part of this work, and a key finding. This also has an important implication from a recovery research perspective. While Humphreys and Lembke (2013) make clear that there is a strong evidence base for peer-delivered interventions, we know much less about the importance of coalitions of professionals, peer and other community members in creating partnerships and resources to support recovery pathways.

What the current project has demonstrated is not only the viability of this model, but also the added value that it confers. In terms of the Christakis and Fowler (2010) approach to social contagion, spread is less likely if there are closed groups and the initiation of a new behavioural epidemic comes from within only one group, particularly if that group is subject to marginalisation and exclusion. The point of a coalition of different kinds of members in this context is specifically to enable the group to access a diverse range of community resources, starting from different networks and different settings in the community. There is also the collective energy derived from the new group and their capacity to influence multiple networks with a clear and positive message to disseminate inclusive attitudes and practices.

This is an area that needs considerably greater research and policy attention that links to the question of what we want from volunteers and 'champions'. The Home Office (2010) makes clear that there is a crucial role for advocates and champions in developing a recovery-oriented system of care but little guidance is offered on how this would work in practice or what this would mean as a career opportunity for people, or what protection and support they would be offered as part of this process. Peer inclusion is an essential component of the social contagion of hope and it is imperative that the needs and support systems are in place to facilitate this model and to ensure that peer champions can flourish with the appropriate guidance and help.

The coalition approach suggests a coming together of diverse groups – people in recovery, people who feel they have completed their recovery journeys, family members, professionals, policy makers and researchers – as well as community activists whose areas of interest are unrelated to substance use. The idea behind this model is simple – that recovery status is not important but that diversity is as central to the aim of the group as it is to have a range of skills (personal capital) and a range of engagements and associations (social capital) that can be shared among the group to increase the overall scale and scope of the project. However, there is also a developmental component through which the group should not only afford volunteers and champions opportunities for network building but also important forms of bridging capital within the connector group. This is part of the reason why the connector navigator group is in itself regarded as an important emerging asset, but not a static one, rather as one that grows and evolves over the course of the project and hopefully significantly beyond. In this way, it is hoped that participation in such a coalition not only instils the benefits of the helper principle in those who take part, but also enables that virtuous circle for all participants.

The challenge, however, is always sustainability and the links this has to issues of resourcing and funding. While the external funders, the Health Foundation, proved to be exceptionally supportive and flexible in promoting and championing the project, the ability to influence local stakeholders to invest beyond the initial stage was much less fruitful. We were not able to get the multi-agency partnership to create local funding sources that would have made the project grow and its activities and successes become embedded as routine practice in local services and provision. And this remains the ultimate objective – the mainstreaming of the connectors model to allow longer-term impacts on community wellbeing to embed and to use the community connections process to fundamentally change the communities for the good.

Key lessons

- The fundamental underlying principle for an effective community partnership is a top-down process that integrates with a bottom-up process to ensure a strategic plan that is guided by community level endeavours and engagement.

- The development of a model like this creates new opportunities at three levels – at the organisational and management level; at the level of teams and workers (improving inter-agency working); and at the level of individuals. Gains at each of these levels will benefit the other levels in the model.

- Identifying and recruiting a diverse group of connectors affords access to an extensive and varied set of local community assets (134 assets were identified in the Sheffield project), and this richness and diversity will grow as the coalition of connectors works together, and their group will become a new asset in its own right.

- Within a month of training up our group of connectors, they were able to form rules and processes to support effective community engagement and start to recruit clients new to recovery to the programme, and these rules helped to guide their efforts and to support them as they engaged externally.

- There was a strong sense of co-production in the project with volunteers and service users actively involved in the development of the project, and shared ownership was key to the success of the project.

- There were strong and sustainable alliances formed at the level of individual clients, across professionals and professional groups and with organisations, generating new linkages and new forms of linking capital.

- Although we struggled to retain an outcome sample, where participants were retained there was clear evidence that the connection led to improvements in personal and social capital and improved engagement with the community, and individual case study reports identified some very strong successes.

- Overall, the project demonstrated the feasibility of coalition working and the benefits of generating partnerships between volunteers, professionals and the community.

7

A visible and accessible recovery community

In this chapter I will focus on one organisation, Double Impact, which has had a profound impact on my thinking about recovery support delivery. It has created a 'hub and spoke' model of visible recovery in Nottingham and in the local area through a commitment to community engagement underpinned by a specific focus on education. What is particularly important for me about this model is how the organisation has engaged with multiple levels of community capital to build social and recovery capital. The chapter starts with an overview of the organisation's history and will then move on to consider the conceptual principles on which it is built before moving on to provide some evidence – and important testimonies – about why this is a strong model and what works in its implementation. The chapter also considers some of the challenges associated with an approach of this kind. This chapter is unusual in that it relies on the testimony of staff and clients to describe the unique characteristics of a service that has generated a long-standing hub of recovery and a foundation for social contagion of hope.

The history and background of Double Impact

Double Impact was founded by Tony Herbert in 1998 and so has been operational for over 20 years. It started as a partnership with a local community college (The People's College) to support recovering drug and alcohol users, and was initially based in the YMCA in Nottingham. Initial funding came in part from the European Social Fund and the initial tranche of funding involved a collaboration with services in Italy, Spain and the Republic of Ireland. Over the course of the next decade the range of services grew as did geographic coverage to extend beyond the city of Nottingham and into the local county of Nottinghamshire, but the organisation retained its primary focus of helping people in recovery into education and employment. By 2006, Double Impact was beginning to develop a national profile with a focus on identifying key factors in effective aftercare through the use of personal development plans for users of the various services. There has always been a focus on personal and individual pathways to recovery sustained by a model of vocational growth and personal development planning.

Momentum continued to grow with the establishment of the Double Impact Volunteering Academy in 2011 and the first Recovery Academy in 2014, with the aim of developing peer mentoring across the county of Nottinghamshire. This is one of 17 educational interventions or activities that Double Impact currently delivers. However, with the opening of Café Sobar, an alcohol-free café and social space in the centre of Nottingham, with offices and group rooms above the café, there is the emergence of a physical and visible hub for recovery. Events include 'Recovery Mondays' aimed specifically at the recovery community, but many of the music and comedy events are designed to target much broader community groups and networks, and the model is based on active community engagement and involvement. In this way, Café Sobar, and Double Impact more generally, combine the goals of supporting bonding capital within the recovery community with creating opportunities for bridging and linking capital beyond it.

Although the meeting rooms are used by a range of local recovery groups including both AA and NA, the café is not overtly targeted at people in recovery and is widely used by shoppers in Nottingham city centre, and provides a safe space for people wanting to avoid the excesses of some of the alternative venues in the evenings. It is important to note that the venue has also been used for meetings and events by organisations as diverse as Nottingham Trent University, Business in the

Community, Amy Winehouse Foundation, The Prince's Trust, Playback Drama Group and St Nic's Church. It has become established as an attractive and engaging venue for a diverse range of community activities. It is also important to note that, within the first year, 31 people in recovery had volunteered in the venue, seven family events had been hosted there and 311 people in recovery had been recorded as participating in social events at Café Sobar. It was also the setting for the first Spirit of Recovery awards event, which now takes place annually. This event is consistent with the idea that celebrating recovery should be a public act of recognition and acclamation that builds recovery visibility and accessibility.

Central to the model of Double Impact has been the twin track of peer-based recovery support and the importance of education and personal development and growth. However, Double Impact has always strived to actively engage a range of stakeholders and community groups, on the one hand, to afford opportunities to its clients and students and, on the other, as part of a process of challenging stigma and actively engaging in community wellbeing and community growth activities in each of the locations in which it has become established. In this way, Double Impact is not committed to any single philosophy of recovery or pathway, but has created an umbrella to support personalised journeys and pathways to positive change.

In this chapter, I will use interview data from key staff at Double Impact as well as case studies from people in long-term recovery who have ongoing contact with the service in one capacity or another. However, before starting to describe what works about Double Impact, there will be a brief review of key conceptual issues that provide the framing for recovery questions that can in part be addressed using this model:

1. How can recovery capital build from social and community engagement?
2. Why do peers have such a central role to play in a process of reintegration and active community engagement?
3. How does the work on education complement the process of peer-based building of personal and social recovery capital?

How Double Impact can contribute to our understanding of recovery models

Building sustainable recovery capital

There are some interesting parallels with JFH in the approach adopted by Double Impact to build sustainable recovery pathways while also contributing to the overall wellbeing of the local community, particularly in Nottingham. Double Impact has always placed a strong emphasis on partnership working – with funders, with education providers, with treatment services, but also with a much more diverse group of community members including the local business community. It is in part as a result of this that the Nottingham Building Society has supported the premises for Café Sobar and the suite of meeting rooms and office space above it and that the Spirit of Recovery awards are possible (in 2018, the Park Plaza Hotel provided the venue and catering free of charge for the event). This is critical not only because it provides much needed resources but also because it generates connections and credibility outside the NGO or treatment sectors and helps to build meaningful and sustainable partnerships. This is similar to the JFH approach to building links to professional groups to access resources directly for the organisation and also to create pathways to community capital for the clients for whom this can be part of their recovery pathway.

Thus, the first key lesson is around social capital and the importance of effective engagement with multiple populations, each of which has access to different kinds of assets, financial, informational, human and so on. Adler (2002: 23) defined social capital as 'the goodwill that is available to individuals or groups. Its source lies in the structure and content of the actor's social relations. Its effects flow from the information, influence and solidarity it makes available to the actor'. What is important here is Putnam's (2000) claim in *Bowling Alone* that it is not the immediate network but friends of friends that help to produce capital, and it is here that there is the clearest connection to the idea of a social contagion. In the current context, this means that people who have limited access to social support can through Double Impact as an organisation, and through its peer mentors on a more personal level, have access to a diverse range of positive resources to support recovery pathways and that can contribute to the growth of hope and empowerment, as well as the practical supports they will need to support their recovery journeys.

As Fukuyama (2001: 8) has argued,

> All groups embodying social capital have a certain radius of trust, that is, the circle of people among whom cooperative norms are operating. If a group's social capital produces positive externalities, the radius of trust can be larger than the group itself.

For Double Impact, the immediate radius of trust is characterised in the groups and physically embedded in Café Sobar, but radiates and permeates through a range of contacts with partners that have access to a much more diverse membership and a resulting diversity of resources in the local communities. This is critical in social capital theory as Coleman (1988) has argued that the poor structures of our communities mean that accessing social capital is difficult, particularly for those who are marginalised or excluded, such as the majority of the client group of Double Impact. In practice, Double Impact aims to create a radius of trust that incorporates a range of external partners to provide access to social capital and community resources to support the recovery journeys of people who have lost or never had sufficient social and community capital to sustain their recovery and to lead a fulfilling and meaningful life. The argument that has been threaded through this book is that accessing those social and community resources creates the space and support needed to build the personal capital – resilience, coping skills, hope and self-efficacy among others – that will allow both recovery and reintegration to become self-sustaining.

One of the key questions that the analysis of Double Impact can answer is around the role of peers in this process. As in many recovery organisations, there is considerable lived experience among the staff and management of Double Impact, and peer support and peer mentoring are essential to the way the organisation functions. This pervades an organisational culture of understanding and empathy that is central to the generation of the radius of trust already outlined.

As Humphreys and Lembke (2013) have concluded, peer-based interventions are critical to the supportive evidence base around recovery and White (2009) has gone further in arguing that the social contagion of recovery is reliant on the role of peers, and that champions of recovery can be described as the 'carriers of recovery'. This notion of contagion is critical to the idea that in a recovery coalition there are important roles for a diversity of partners – professionals, friends and family members, community representatives and community members – but that other people in recovery have a distinctive role. As Moos (2007) has argued, peer champions have two critical social roles, both in providing a role model of how to do recovery, but also in providing support and guidance in learning what the values, norms and beliefs are about living in recovery.

This has been central to the effectiveness of the 12-step fellowships where the idea of sponsorship is based on this combined idea of a more experienced member taking on the role of role model and guide, and of the mentors themselves growing and developing as a part of this process. However, and very much in contrast to the anonymity of the 12-step fellowships, a recovery hub like Café Sobar is highly visible and accessible to ensure that individuals are attracted and actively engaged, and the role modelling of effective and collective recovery plays a key role in the contagion of recovery ideas and beliefs. There is nothing incompatible about these objectives – people can even attend 12-step meetings in the Double Impact building above Café Sobar, and can make their own personal choices about how overt they are about their recovery. As we have seen in the chapter on JFH, the aim of making a recovery project visible and accessible is based on the concept of social contagion and that celebrating success and achievement will make this journey successively easier for each subsequent group and generation. As recovery success stories proliferate they become more visible and normalised, and create a pathway for those struggling to make this transition, and who may question whether recovery is possible.

In addition, the hub creates the conditions for a 'therapeutic landscape for recovery' (Wilton and DeVerteuil, 2006). Based on work in a town called San Pedro in California, the authors demonstrated that the growth of a visible recovery community led not only to improved bonding capital within a growing recovery community, but also greater bridging capital as the links to the wider community grew challenging stigma and exclusion. By providing a safe alcohol and drug free space in the centre of Nottingham, Café Sobar has created a space that not only promotes increased bonds within the recovery community, but an attractive and accessible window to recovery for those striving for it and for the wider community in the city. It makes recovery visible and accessible to new groups and populations by building bridges between a range of local groups and individuals and an engaging, attractive and accessible form of recovery.

One of the fundamental objectives here is to challenge stigma and exclusion. Drug use is the most stigmatised health condition in the world according to the World Health Organization (2001), with alcohol the fourth most stigmatised, as the general public holds stereotyped and negative views, considering people who use drugs as: lacking self-discipline and willpower (Jones et al, 2010); and 'dirty' and disrespectful towards themselves and others (Sloan, 2012; see also Hughes, 1999). Increased contact between the public and stigmatised groups generally results in lessening of stigma. Just as importantly, however, it creates a safe space for the promotion of bridging recovery capital and for championing the broader social justice values of recovery as a social movement for change.

Café Sobar is situated in the centre of Nottingham and has been designed to be highly engaging and attractive.

There is space for a stage and it is used regularly in the evenings for concerts and other public events designed to provide social activities for people in recovery but also for people not in recovery looking for a safe social space. This is the setting for a therapeutic landscape in which recovery is subtly woven into the signs and symbols of the café and where recovery is pervasive but not invasive to patrons who may be unaware of its provenance. This also provides a structured set of social activities for people in recovery to engage in positive and pro-social activities free from the risk and temptation of alcohol.

The café is effectively the 'front of house' component of a recovery hub that has also developed a strong tradition around the importance of education in recovery. This brings us to the next key theme and question around Double Impact, which relates to the role of education. In his key text, 'Pathways from the culture of addiction to the culture of recovery', White (1996) discusses the transition to recovery as involving multiple zones of action. The five zones he identifies are physical, psychological, spiritual, lifestyle and relationship. Each involves a search for wholeness and a reconstruction of personal values. For many people this will require a period of exploration and personal re-definition and one of the key areas around this involves education and 'self-improvement'.

A recent report (Clinks and Social Firms UK, 2014) has looked at ex-offenders who had established social enterprises, considering how their learning could inform and assist others in creating their own employment. The report identifies several barriers including a lack of formal qualifications, literacy and numeracy difficulties, and a lack of work history. In the sections that follow, I summarise interview materials from meetings with a number of Double Impact (DI) staff and case studies before drawing some themes and conclusions from this work.

Interviews with staff about what works in Double Impact

I am extremely grateful for the time and input of a number of staff and managers who have been extremely supportive of this project and my work more generally, and what I present in the next section is a summary of their perceptions and experiences of working at DI.

Café Sobar

The manager of the café suggested that

> 'Sobar benefits from volunteers in recovery by having a small unpaid staff team to support the

> operation and more importantly individuals provide a human contact directly to the recovery community. Individuals also inform the staff team who are not in recovery about the recovery community from a lived experience perspective as opposed to a theoretical one. This also provides a positive link directly to the recovery events that occur at Sobar therefore informing their development.'

There is a clear pathway from early recovery to voluntary activities and then potentially paid employment in the café but simply being there provides an opportunity to actively engage with different aspects of the recovery community, through its role as a local hub for recovery. The manager of the café went on to say that "I know of four volunteers who have gone on to work in the Sobar on a full and part time basis", meaning that it is a pathway to employment as well as to social and community engagement. This can happen because it has attempted to reconcile the roles of recovery hub and a successful business from the outset. As a senior manager at DI has argued,

> 'It has become a hub over time – it took a while – it was never just a hub for recovery – it was a high street business – hard to merge its identity as a recovery hub with generating enough of an income to keep going. Identity as a recovery hub has emerged slowly – helped by the fact there is a room for hire for MA fellowships from day one – from day one that happened with AA meetings taking place in the building.'

There is also a sense in which Café Sobar affords the opportunity for these two functions to come together. One of the senior managers went on to suggest that,

> 'The Café has become a venue for social activity to take place – around those regular weekly fixtures – "the meeting after the meeting" – social support after the meeting. That's when the newcomers get

> together, talk about what is going on outside the meeting, build friendships and acquaintances. On Sundays, there are two meetings, and on Friday there are two meetings.'

In this way, there is a structure for formal recovery groups, supported by a space and place for the essential social engagement opportunities that can build relationships and the social capital essential to support the recovery journey and pathway. As one of the senior managers said, this is not only to create bonds within the recovery community but bridges to wider social groups:

> 'We have endeavoured to put on social activities for people in recovery have tried to make them as accessible to anyone in recovery, a friend, family members – regular recovery events – live music, comedy, live poetry, open mic stuff – not all of whom are in recovery, but a fair percentage are.'

Another senior manager reported that

> 'Café Sobar has been brilliant for the profile and credibility of Double Impact both locally and further afield. I think that the perception of Double Impact has changed, in a way it's given us more credibility and substance. Because we have established a high profile venue in the city centre which is run in a professional way it is hard not to be impressed! We get people from across the country contacting us and wanting to visit, and in a way seeing Café Sobar and Double Impact as an example of best practice and something they aspire to have in their locality. Likewise Double Impact has been able to use Café Sobar as our "shop window" and we have had numerous meetings with commissioners and national drug and alcohol treatment providers at the venue.'

In this sense, Café Sobar has become a clear recovery beacon that has not only built recovery resource in the city of Nottingham, it has also become an exemplar of how recovery can be showcased and made viable and accessible to a wide range of groups and organisations, as well as to individuals. However, the focus remains on sustainability with one manager, Stephen Youdell, going on to say,

> 'first and foremost Café Sobar has to be a self-sufficient business in its own right that is competing in a highly competitive marketplace. Having said that, we do use Café Sobar's online presence to nudge conversation to Double Impact and the work we do.'

Stephen was also very clear that in doing so, it has become an important and sustainable hub for the recovery community.

> 'The local AA fellowship have established six meetings a week in the meeting room attached to the Café. This has enabled a visible recovery community to become established at the venue, this in turn has introduced more of the recovery community to the work of Double Impact which has resulted in both referrals to access our services and individuals wishing to volunteer for Double Impact. Café Sobar has also become a destination for a wide range of other community groups who use the venue on a regular basis, not only is this helping to break down stigma but also raising the profile of the work we do and the availability of our services to a wider audience.'

Stephen concluded that

> 'Café Sobar has challenged stigma, we believe it is okay to be in recovery from addiction and don't shy away from championing that, it's not something to be ashamed about. Likewise we don't feel we have to have signs on the wall ramming it down people's throats. We have created a visible link between Café Sobar and Double Impact if you look for it!'

Double Impact Academy

Throughout its history DI has had a strong focus on education and employment, and this tradition is now embodied in the Recovery Academy. The aims of the DI Academy (identified on its website, https://www.doubleimpact.org.uk/how-we-help/education-employment/) are:

- to connect people with themselves, each other and their local communities;
- to raise aspirations and ambition;
- to access key functional skills training where needed;
- to access level 1 and 2 progression learning;
- to coordinate volunteering and work experience opportunities;
- to support students to be work ready and into employment;
- to generate a Peer Support network;
- to develop a service user involvement network; and
- to promote and champion recovery.

The problem faced in the UK is that educational programmes are either focused on basic literacy and competence or formal qualifications for people who want to work in the drug and alcohol field, as counsellors or peer workers. So the Recovery Academy aims to give people an initial step on the educational ladder, if they need it, provide the support to help those clients achieve, and then look to develop and support their ongoing educational activities and needs.

The chief executive of DI, Graham Miller, explained the underlying principle of the Academy as

> 'what DI has always tried to do is to create virtual network points. People can move back and forward, linking into wider communities – with the Academy, it is a network point to the wider world of education. They can experience the world of education and it can lead to effective transitions – DI gives the structure and support.'

Graham puts forward the argument that recovery progression is not linear but is about creating networks and contacts that can inspire change and active engagement in education as in other pathways to recovery.

In terms of the history of the organisation, education was a core goal from the very start. As Graham explained,

> 'People want to learn who have never been at school since the age of 12 or 13. Other people would want to retrain or reskill in other areas of work. At the time [when DI started], IT was really moving at a pace and people in our services were being left behind. Nobody had laptops – the first course we ever ran was IT skills.'

Within a framework of personal development, the Academy has the twin aims of providing skills to those who have never had education and offering re-skilling to those looking for new skills and abilities. This is not only for those who have had little prior education, but also for those whose educational experiences were some time in the past, for whom technological barriers to learning need to be overcome as part of the process.

However, Graham went on to explain the underlying model as

> 'it is not so much about the academic stuff we deliver, it is much more about the way we have delivered that education. it is about the settings and the quality of staff no matter what the subject matter. When it comes to the Academy, Rachel – who leads the QA [quality assurance] on all of the Academy – it is all about transformational learning.'

This would be consistent with the broader notion of social and group pathways to recovery where there is a strong interpersonal relationship and this is embedded within a group that provides safety, support and direction for people in early recovery. Another of the senior managers at DI, Eleanor, picked up the thread in suggesting that,

> 'People need a structure and something to do with their time and if you are not setting out to be a therapeutic service, you are looking at learning in its broadest sense. We have always bridged academic and practical learning – and we have continued doing this because it works.'

The key concept for DI staff is that they are an aftercare provider whose role is to support individuals to move on with their lives and this requires effective engagement with the community.

Graham went on to conclude that "You are using learning to give people a new identity – and to develop the networks to flourish underneath that and it all glues together". This fits with the adapted CHIME In Action model presented in Chapter 8, in which Connections to the recovery community inspire Hope, which provides the drive and the motivation for people to initiate that cyclical process of changed Identity through having a sense of Meaning in their lives, which is Empowering and inspiring. This is the point that Graham made about networks – they provide the initial inspiration that generates hope, which creates a belief that there is a viable change option and that it can be realised through active engagement with community assets and the people who are embedded in each of these assets. Visible and attractive recovery hubs can attract people in and inspire and support the process of change.

The Academy programme is much more geographically diverse than Café Sobar and is located in each of the centres run by DI in the East Midlands, but the clients from each of those services are encouraged and even supported to come into Café Sobar to experience the recovery hub and to develop their own recovery contacts and connections.

The experiences of volunteers and staff at DI

This first quotation comes from one of the staff at Café Sobar:

> 'What I get from volunteering at Sobar café is many things on many levels. I don't have many times in my daily life, when I am free from the white noise and

> nonsense of my mind or emotions, but here with the team I get relief from it. I have only recognised two points of panic whilst working here, which is amazing given my fear of people and their proximity to me, and how normally I would experience panic multiple times a day. I can't begin to tell you how much being able to work here has helped me challenge away so many boundaries and limitations I have in my life and how much I can see the strength in me growing.'

This is a core role of a recovery hub – it can be seen as a place of calm, of safety and of serenity, providing a refuge and a safe haven for people in recovery. However, it does so in a way that challenges them to extend their boundaries and to move out of their comfort zones.

As Eleanor, the manager, has argued,

> 'Over a few years we ran arts projects, to take people out there to different venues, to galleries, cinemas, theatre – taking part in what the city has to offer. This is a principle we try to put into the pathway. Otherwise, people get stuck in services and don't want to leave. Some people want to use the services as a day centre forever and a day.'

In other words, the service aims to provide a place of comfort and safety but also to be a resource that will challenge them to grow and develop. This is also the point at which bonding and bridging capital are essential – the bonds within the group form a core part of emerging recovery capital but they require bridges to new individuals, groups and communities to continue to flourish and to maximise human potential. The emphasis here is on continual growth and preventing the risk of stagnation in recovery pathways and journeys.

Eleanor concluded that

> 'Café Sobar is a good way of getting people to risks but with support and protection – all the bars and pubs round about. We have had to work hard – it is

> easy for people in recovery to cocoon themselves. You have to work with it in the early stages of recovery, they do need protection and a safe place – and this comes up continuously in feedback. But you often have to take the lead in encouraging people to extend their boundaries.'

For this reason, the reconciliation of working internally to support growth and build a supportive and strong recovery community has gone hand in hand with the idea of linking to external groups to create pathways and to support recovery integration into the wider community. What is distinctive about Café Sobar and the Academy is that they have created strong and visible recovery communities that create hope and connection for people at various stages of the recovery journey and that support and encourage community engagement.

Simon's story

As much as possible, the case studies are presented to represent the voice of the narrator and not my own. They were typed as the person narrated their story and so mistakes are likely to represent my failures rather than those of the individuals whose stories they represent. Simon was asked a basic set of six questions that form the core of his recovery story, starting with an overview of how he got into trouble with addiction in the first place:

> 'A fairly classic story – I didn't feel I fitted in. I had a disrupted family – I had a twin brother: I lived with one parent and he lived with the other. I was kicked out of a few schools. At 15, I found cannabis and alcohol and this just made me feel better. I pursued that for a number of years. I guess that once I had opened the floodgates to one substance I was more willing to try others but my main substances were alcohol and cannabis. My mental health was not good and by the time I got into my 30s my life was a complete mess, and I ended up on heroin and

> crack. I felt trapped and unable to get out of that. I had much less contact with family, extremely isolated and almost agoraphobic.'

As is often the case, the path to recovery does not reveal itself quickly and Simon reported that

> 'at that point, about 34, I first started to look for help. I was given the number for an NA helpline and met people there who introduced me to DI. I felt broken and absolutely hopeless – I can't live like this anymore. I had no friends and no hope – I was crippled with anxiety. I had to see the doctor for antidepressants and they weren't working. I wanted to escape how I felt about my life. There was a pay-off – eventually alcohol and drugs stopped giving me anything – I just felt more anxious, paranoid and I heard voices – life was just unbearable – I was so desperate to get out, I phoned my mum and that was how I started. I didn't stay clean initially – it took a few years.'

What helped Simon, in his own words, was

> 'Going to 12-step fellowship and to DI – people seemed to understand how I was feeling. They had similar enough lives, I started to feel that I belonged for the first time ever. I had a lot of support – in my mid-30s I made the first friends I had ever had in my life. People would gather round you and give you support – initially I was a little suspicious. At that time, I was going to NA meetings on a daily basis, I had a keyworker at DI and I would pop in there for a coffee – there was quite a lot of socialising. Initially, that was really difficult as I could hardly have a conversation because of anxiety. Then I started to exercise more – walking, cycling. For the first time I had a timetable that I was sticking to – I wasn't just using. And also for the first time, I had fun and I laughed a lot.'

When asked about the role that DI had played in his recovery journey, Simon said

> 'A keyworker really believed in me – he just stuck with me, when I didn't believe in myself. He showed me that I could do it – he was really encouraging and supportive. He helped me set some goals. And then there was the voluntary work – although only initially three hours a week, it was a foot in the door of employment and I hadn't worked for eight or nine years. I couldn't believe how important that was to me – that people would trust me to sit on the reception. They also gave me counselling about family stuff. But the main feature was constant support while I was bouncing around. One-to-one sessions, groups and volunteering was core. I now have part-time support work to role model recovery work but also for people who have been in services for a period of time to signpost them – and I love it!'

There is very clear evidence here for the amended CHIME In Action model proposed in this book – that connections generate belonging and a sense of hope but they also open doors to opportunities, which in Simon's case took the form of voluntary work. This is generative for him – the feeling of trust and inclusion leads to improvements in self-esteem and self-efficacy and an emerging sense of pride that is linked to a new identity. Part of the connection is bridging and linking capital that mobilises community capital through new social connections. This is the virtuous circle of desistance and recovery and is apparent in his concluding comments about where he saw his life at the time of the interview:

> 'My life is the best it has ever been – I was 21 months clean last week. I am doing a Health and Social Care Level 3 at university; I got my twin brother to go to his first meeting yesterday, and I am back with my family. I genuinely feel that I had a second chance at life. Things are not always easy – but I believe that

> everything is doable. If you come through addiction and survive it, you are made of some pretty strong stuff. I want to make my family proud and help others. That is why I go to DI – I still go to meetings and work for DI – and that is why.'

This sense of being someone who can make other people proud, can help other people and can contribute is a key dynamic in the process of change, and the role of DI is both about triggering the start of this journey and then nurturing and supporting along the road.

However, Simon is clear in his own conclusion about the role of DI in his journey:

> 'DI really gets this idea of a recovery community and it feels like a family, and it always seemed like a safe place to go. Sometimes, when I was struggling I would go in and I always knew there would be someone to speak to. I genuinely believe it saved my life. I didn't think I could have done my recovery in another city – DI played such a big role.'

As with the role of the therapist, so recovery support services can have that twin role to perform – first to encourage people that change is possible, and then to follow that up by providing ongoing support and guidance, with both stages underpinned by effective linkage and genuine human bonds and care. What is important about Simon's story is that while he credits DI with a very important role, he is clear about his own transition and the growth in his own personal capital when he refers to being made of "pretty strong stuff".

Conclusions and overview

DI offers a distinctive insight into the workings of an effective recovery hub that provides a strong space for both bonding and bridging capital. Overall, the organisation has developed from a single site in the centre of Nottingham to a number of regional sites, but the focal point has increasingly become around the café in the centre of the city and the educational programme that operates from each of the regional teams.

As the management staff have indicated, the focus has been on creating an authentic 'high street café' which is commercially viable, while also creating a safe hub for both the recovery community and for people looking for an alcohol-free venue in the centre of the city. The building also has separate space for recovery meetings and groups, and the café acts as a meeting place before and after a range of mutual aid meetings. What it has achieved, and what is reflected in the recovery stories presented in this chapter, is the balance of supporting the recovery community while engaging with both business in the city and with the general public. It is through this model that it has achieved both bridging and bonding social capital, and this has prevented the café from becoming a closed setting for people in recovery. Instead, it is widely recognised by the people of Nottingham as a safe space to go, which is attractive and engaging and free from alcohol and drugs.

It has also provided opportunities for volunteering and employment that have been critical in our case studies and which reflect the relationship between personal and social capital growth in recovery. As our first case study illustrates, working in the café provides both space from external stresses and pressures and the opportunity to engage and interact with a diverse group of the general public, in the safety of a prescribed role, that of waitress or barista. Café Sobar also provided a gathering point for recovery community events that were not specific to any particular recovery model or philosophy nor only to those with direct lived experience (and so could involve family members and friends), reflecting an inclusivity that is essential for the growth of a recovery community and championing a social justice model.

This ties in well with the focus on education when considered more broadly in the context of personal development, with DI having a very clear focus on the notion of progression and development, epitomised by the Recovery Academy. Thus there is a clear aim of helping people to develop personal recovery capital through a range of educational attainments and opportunities, but these are supplemented and embedded in a fundamentally relational world where both peer and therapeutic relationships are critical to the effectiveness of the model. One of the reasons for DI's success is around providing a range of supports that will address different needs across the time window of the recovery journey, and then providing access to partners who can help to realise educational and vocational goals. The education is not seen as an end in itself but as a stepping stone to further milestones and achievements.

One of the other key features of DI is its commitment to peer support with a high proportion of the staff having a lived experience, although this is not made manifest if it is not required. This ensures ongoing pathways to helper and volunteer status for the peer mentors, many of whom may eventually get paid work with the organisation, but also provides a reservoir of role models and recovery navigators for those new to their recovery journeys. This is a core part of the personal development component where there is a clear and viable pathway to meaningful and sustainable employment that can also build connections within the recovery community as well as bridges to other groups that have access to a range of community resources and opportunities.

At the heart of this is the relational component with strong and shared bonds between the senior staff (who also have a heritage dating back to the start of the organisation), between staff and clients, and between clients at different stages of their recovery journey. This is Fukuyama's (2001) notion of a radius of trust, with hope emanating from the connections within DI because there is a solid foundation of trust underpinning these relationships. At the heart of this model is the notion of individualised and personalised pathways within a shared commitment to common values of personal growth, wellbeing and positive relationships, whether they are within groups or in one-to-one relationships. There is a strong and palpable sense of community and connectedness at DI that translates into shared values and a commitment to supporting multiple recovery pathways.

The radius of trust generated by DI is important because it acts as a form of community engagement and external partnership that impacts on the local community and creates bridges to a number of community organisations. It is this part of the model that creates dynamism and sustainability as it is from here that effective engagement with the local community can emerge.

Key lessons

- Double Impact is an important peer model based on developing a radius of trust and creating a strong sense of community for people at various stages of recovery, based around a visible recovery hub that has created the environment for both bonding and bridging capital.
- At the heart of the DI model of recovery are education and personal development, with the Recovery Academy championing the idea that recovery can grow through building self-esteem and self-efficacy via personalised pathways to positive change.
- This concept of a hub and spoke model means that there is a central point for coming together for events and activities, and a localised service that makes recovery support accessible and available.
- DI's growth has championed a form of partnership with local organisations and businesses that has helped to make DI sustainable but has also provided resources and supports for their clients.
- DI's strength has been around belonging and connection and is a wonderful example of recovery growth and development as a shared journey of partnership and trust.

8

Overview and conclusions

As I stated at the start of the book, the projects described here are all unique and innovative but they are not the only projects around community connections that fall into this category. They were all selected opportunistically because they represent the embodiment of my understanding of recovery as a personal and individual journey but one that is embedded firmly in social and societal processes of change and growth. For that reason, what is reviewed in this final chapter is by no means final or definitive but exemplifies key aspects of supportive models of recovery that are embedded in the local community. Once the chapters have been reviewed, some of the key lessons will be outlined and the broader implications for policy and practice considered, and the key foundations for a model of social recovery described.

Essentially this closing chapter is a synthesis of the knowledge garnered from the six data chapters as the concept of building community capital is developed through increasingly refined questions and outlined as a process to support the mobilisation of community resources and the building of community linkage methods. It also involves a lessons learned section, and this includes the introduction of material and evidence from the US and Europe to critically appraise our knowledge about communities and the conceptual model presented, which is in effect a summation of what I have observed in these projects and the other desistance and recovery research I have carried out over the past 15 years. While each chapter has identified problems and barriers (and how they were overcome), the final chapter contains a section on some of the challenges that may arise and what lessons were learned about attempting to overcome resistance and barriers.

Review of the key processes and findings

The earliest studies were from Australia where the inspiration, vision and commitment of key individuals in a therapeutic community and a Magistrates Court provided the inspiration and motivation that allowed the initial ideas to be put into practice. The first project in partnership with the magistrates from Dandenong Magistrates Court used the asset mapping model to address an issue around repeat offending among young people with substance use issues in a deprived area of Melbourne. This mapping exercise demonstrated that, even in areas with relatively low social cohesion and considerable frictions and challenges, there are a myriad of assets that can be identified. In some ways this was not a surprise. What was more of a surprise was that many of the key individuals in these agencies, interest groups and community organisations were willing and positive about engaging with the courts and their client group. In some ways, this was the initial spark for the idea of a contagion of hope. Further, the process of engaging and mobilising these groups generated a sense of momentum and hope in its own right.

The second Australian study came about through the endeavours of a senior manager in the Salvation Army from the Eastern Division of Australia, Gerard Byrne, who wanted to rethink the notion of how therapeutic communities work to create a 'TC without walls' – a vibrant and active participant in its local community. As a result of this commitment, two TCs on the central coast, Dooralong and Fairhaven, became involved in a project which focused on two activities: creating an asset map and then developing a systematic model for operationalising those assets – the first attempt to be systematic around active community connections. The project also involved an early 'coalition' between current staff, graduates of the programme and current clients of the two services. This also initiated the idea that there were assets inside the TC, and outside the TC, and that effective connections require a combination of the two, with an explicit aim of benefiting all of those potentially involved. These two projects provided both clear evidence for the feasibility of the model and the beginning of a method that has been developed in subsequent chapters. The spread of benefit to the community at large and beyond addiction recovery really was the foundation for the idea of social contagion of hope and what ultimately developed into recovery cities.

However, to return to chronological order, the idea of asset mapping was not a central component of the JFH approach but it was crucial to its effective application. The central idea of the JFH model was to help disenfranchised individuals, primarily people in early recovery coming out of either addiction treatment or prison, to find a safe place to live and to develop a range of professional skills and capabilities, while building up strong recovery networks, that subsequently evolved into access to a diverse range of community resources. Central to the JFH model was the idea of social capital – both bonding and bridging, and the importance of connections to multiple groups. The primary engagement strategy for JFH was around bonding capital – with a strong sense of engagement and commitment encouraged between the apprentices and the staff, and a significant resource investment in ensuring a range of pro-social activities outside of working hours. This helped to create a clear JFH identity, supported by the distinctive and visible clothing, signage and branding associated with the social enterprise.

In the JFH project, we were also able to extend the range and scope of the evaluation methods to increase the sensitivity of the analysis. One of the most important aspects of this was the use of social media, first as part of the JFH support process and then as it contributed to the evaluation method. The staff started a Facebook page for JFH apprentices to provide them with information about recovery activities and events but this rapidly became a communication mechanism and a support system for those involved in the project. As this was an open page, it also afforded us the opportunity to analyse the impact of engagement with social media, with fascinating results (Best et al, 2018; Bliuc et al, 2017). The findings were strongly supportive of recovery theory and of social identity approaches (Best et al, 2016). Those who were retained longer in JFH had better outcomes, but crucially what predicted staying longer was being more central to the online network, identifying with the group (more use of 'we' than 'I' in posts) and being endorsed more often by other people. Thus, there was a strong sense of dynamic engagement where belonging leads to endorsement which in turn creates more robust bonds which helps to retain clients and so improves the stability of their recovery journeys. This is a key part of the story as it supports the idea that belonging to a group is important to engagement with it, while also offering us a new and innovative way (that is not intrusive) to measure how effectively this happens. The use of a Facebook page by a recovery group is another sign of innovation and flexibility in providing support and its uptake by the clients is strongly suggestive of the potential importance social media can play in holistic recovery engagement and support.

The second core part of the JFH story is about external engagement. JFH was not only successful because the apprentices were strongly bonded to each other and to the staff (which would be described as bonding capital) through a shared vision of recovery as a process of gaining pride and dignity through work and through giving something back to the community with the housing work that was at the heart of the project. They were also afforded links to a diverse range of groups and communities in Blackpool, including recovery groups but also involving arts and drama, education and training, and unusually the building trade and the business community in the town. In this way, JFH did not merely replicate the asset mapping and utilisation model described in Australia, it amended the approach to take full advantage of the resources that were available to it and the connections the organisation already had. Thus, tradespeople who were business contacts for the social enterprise not only were able to offer jobs to some of the apprentices, they were also supportive of JFH events and provided access to a range of community resources that might well have been denied the group otherwise.

This is reflected in the social media analysis which shows that while the staff and apprentices occupy the centre of the social network, there is considerable interaction with a diverse range of external stakeholders – evidence of bridging capital to a number of professional groups and community organisations in Blackpool and throughout the country. JFH challenged exclusion and stigma through a process of reintegration based not only on the working endeavours of the team but on the active involvement with multiple community groups and activities that forced engaged individuals to change their views and to take pride in this local initiative which spread hope and belief about the town as well as the individuals involved.

The key inference from the JFH programme of work is that a group of people with multiple disadvantages, including histories of substance use and criminal justice involvement, were able to support each other and to garner support from the wider community in an area that would not be considered as opportune for supporting recovery or high in community cohesion or community resources. It is against this background that the subsequent project, with HMP Kirkham, should be considered. Most of the prisoners at Kirkham are from this economically deprived area yet we were able to implement a programme of work based around hope and trust, with active support and engagement from multiple stakeholder groups who would not normally be expected to work together as a recovery coalition.

The evaluation of JFH and the commitment of the prison governor, Graham Beck, to this type of inclusive, strengths-based working created the initial partnership on which the Kirkham partnership was based. This senior strategic commitment was crucial in overcoming some of the initial staffing anxieties around governance and risk around attempting to engage family members in the process of community engagement. The project itself was intrinsically relational, reliant on an equal partnership between prisoners, family members and prison staff, working together to identify both community resources and opportunities and the mechanisms for engaging effectively with them. There was also a clear objective that the radius of trust generated by the project would spread further throughout the prison.

The literature would suggest that both prisoners and family members are typically lacking in social capital and under significant pressure (Codd, 2007; Comfort, 2003), yet there was a high level of support and engagement for the current project with increasing enthusiasm from the prisoner cohort about engaging and encouraging family members to participate in the project. However, it was the engagement of the probation team and their experience of a sense of 're-awakening' of their professional values that was unique and crucial to the project. The benefits of strengths-based working were apparent in the emerging partnership and the growth of trust and commitment within the group. One of the key additions that will have to be made in future evaluations of the connectors programme will be around social cohesion and commitment.

This experience was at the heart of the title of this book – a real sense of a social contagion of hope that spread through all three groups who took part (as well as my evaluation team), with a genuine ripple effect throughout the prison and out into the community. While it is far too early to talk about efficacy and outcome impact, the process is generative and builds trust and belief both in dyads and across the groups, and as such poses challenges for researchers who are trying to quantify such things. In other words, the hope has a contagious effect that inspires positive engagement and commitment and a sense of social identity. Another important discovery from this programme was that the process is as important as the outcome, as it created a belief in the rehabilitative model and the viability of strengths-based working as a way of improving not only the prisoner experience but also the working lives of prison staff.

This relates to the idea that recovery takes place on three levels: as a personal journey to wellbeing and belonging; as a social process of positive and valued relationships; and as a social movement that creates a sense of pride and positive identity. From this springs the idea of recovery as a process of embedding social justice that was manifest in the creation of SARRG and the subsequent emergence of the idea of recovery cities. Behind the development of SARRG was the idea that researching recovery could be a positive and empowering experience for addiction professionals and for people in recovery, while also contributing to a growing social movement.

The idea of four key recovery events each year were part of a commitment to a visible celebration of recovery that was designed to create a positive and accessible social identity, and to challenge exclusion and stigma. However, events such as the annual recovery bike ride were also designed to be fun for all of those taking part and to help blur the distinctions between people in recovery, their families, professionals, researchers and academics, and others supportive of the event and the activity. The aim was to make recovery something that was fun, attractive and inclusive, irrespective of what recovery philosophy individuals adhered to or whether they were recovered, in recovery or a family member. This approach created social capital in the form of bonds and bridges, but also generated new social capital in the form of the group who came together to organise and celebrate each event and activity. Sheffield is now recognised both academically and in community terms as a centre for recovery and this can only help us to grow a model of inclusion and participation.

And this has implications for wider issues of social justice that have informed our work in the neighbouring city of Doncaster. Based on a partnership with a dynamic and proactive recovery treatment service with a strong and charismatic lead, Stuart Green, Doncaster has developed a reputation for innovation and the annual Recovery Games attracts interest and participation from all over the UK. The event has grown year on year and is now a significant part of the recovery calendar, attracting teams from all over the country, who are there to compete, to socialise, to have fun but above all to celebrate what is possible in recovery. Therefore, this was the ideal location for the notion of a recovery city predicated on the idea from ROSC (Kelly and White, 2011) that strategic leadership needs to be combined with ground level activity to create an effective model for sustainable change.

In partnership with European Cities Against Drugs (ECAD) and the cities of Ghent and Gothenburg, the aim of recovery cities is to use the contagion of hope associated with recovery groups and communities as a mechanism to challenge stigma and exclusion at a community level. The idea is to identify and share learning and knowledge across multiple cities but to go beyond addiction recovery to include people desisting from offending and on to include all marginalised and excluded groups in an initiative to make communities more connected and more inclusive.

Based on the principles of restorative cities, the aim is to champion recovery models across Europe and share lessons about how to deliver effective recovery models and approaches. This remains a work in progress, but there is considerable interest in the idea that championing recovery for one vulnerable and excluded group (drug and alcohol users) can create increased social capital in communities (based on the idea that using social capital can increase rather than decrease the total stock of capital available). The aim is to use this approach to improve bridging and linking capital across communities to increase civic participation, community cohesion and the wellbeing and health of all members of the community. Challenging exclusion and stigma is undertaken through strengths-based working and is based on the principles of contagion and trust.

Our first attempt to achieve this at a city level is in Sheffield where we undertook the Community Connectors project, funded by the Health Foundation, and in partnership with Sheffield City Council, SHSC and SASS. The aim of the project was to engage and train a group of people established in their own recovery to act as community connectors and to support people at the start of their recovery journey to make effective connections into recovery groups and communities. The first stage was highly successful with 21 community connectors recruited from across volunteers and professional staff from addiction treatment services and even one or two of our own students. As with previous connections and engagement projects, one of the main successes was in creating a vibrant and strong group that developed a commitment to the project and its principles, but also towards the group and to each other. For some of the people in the group who were in recovery, this project afforded a chance to learn from both the university academics and the addiction professionals around issues of ethics, governance and delivery of interventions, but the learning was reciprocal and shared in a spirit of trust and group commitment. But this project, as with both of the projects in Australia, also carry a warning that is around legacy and sustainability and the risks where projects are tied to particular pieces of funding that achievements made can be lost just as quickly.

There was, nonetheless, a significant success in the Health Foundation Community Connectors project engagement of community organisations across a diverse range of topics and activities, with more than 130 groups successfully engaged as connections, building on existing links and establishing new networks and connections. As with previous exercises, these were divided across the areas of sport and recreation, education and training, community and volunteering, and mutual aid, and they were spread geographically across the city and the surrounding area. This meant a strong foundation for matching the individual needs of people in early recovery based on their enthusiasms, skills and capabilities, all with the aim of building recovery capital, first social and community, and then personal. One of the key concepts within the model presented in this book is that recovery is a personal journey that builds strengths and capabilities, but that these are generally acquired through social mechanisms and through community engagement.

This is the idea of scaffolding and is based on a reading of the recovery evidence that suggests the reason for the long-term journey to recovery is that individuals need to grow and to learn from others and to be accepted and integrated back into families, communities and structures like work and housing. What the connections model offers, and what is explored in Chapter 6 is that, while clients can experience this growth, change occurs at four different levels:

1. Clients who are excluded and isolated and have low social capital are provided with support to engage with active recovery resources and a range of wider community assets that can improve their recovery capital.
2. Those further on in their recovery journeys have the opportunity to grow and to give back while benefiting from the helper principle and increasing their own bonds and bridges into the local community. They can also extend their own social networks, community capital and sense of active belonging to their communities.
3. One of the most important findings of this study, as with all of the previous studies, is the creation of a 'coalition' of community connectors and recovery champions, which in turn becomes a new form of asset. It is for this reason that the process is emphasised in community connections work – there is an iterative process of evolution and growth that

can create new structures and groups, as well as promoting the social contagion of hope. The group has strong bonding capital for its members and can develop a series of new bridges to other groups and communities.

4. Finally, and one of the most important lessons from the Sheffield Connectors project, was the growth in connections and engagement among professional organisations and their staff. While they were also influenced by the positive and strengths-based approach, there were also improved engagement and connections at all levels from volunteers through to senior executives. Not only through the role of volunteers, staff are a key part of any recovery-oriented system and their connections, wellbeing and participation in positive events and groups is an essential element of an effective recovery model.

These are 'added value' components of strengths-based work that are often hard to capture quantitatively but are essential to the spreading of hope. Although the number of clients new to recovery successfully engaged was relatively low, the overall process was one of growth and emergence of partnership and connections. We now switch to a focus on what can be learned from the various studies and projects presented and what implications this has for a social model of recovery.

CHIME revisited

To briefly review this work, Leamy et al (2011) reviewed the mental health recovery literature and concluded that there were five essential elements in recovery supportive programmes that fulfilled the acronym CHIME: Connectedness; Hope; Identity; Meaning and Empowerment. The evidence presented in the original review is that these are 'essential elements' in an effective recovery programme. However, our argument will go beyond that in terms of recovery from addiction and will suggest a sequence and order to how these factors coalesce to support positive change. In the model we put forward here the client level model would support the initial sequence – it is connections that promote hope – through observing successful recovery transitions and the recognition that recovery is possible. But connections to positive and pro-social groups also offer new group belonging and a resulting identity change, based on the model I outlined with colleagues in SIMOR (Best et al, 2016).

There are two significant implications of this process. The first is that changes in group membership bring about changes in identity through a process of social identification with the new group. As we engage with attractive and appealing groups that we want to be a part of, we subtly shift our discourse, behaviours and beliefs to fall into line with the attitudes and values of the group. Not only do we know that the more groups a person belongs to, the more protected they are in terms of health and wellbeing (Jetten et al, 2012a), but this only applies when those groups have positive social value (Jetten et al, 2015). Thus, creating manageable and accessible pathways to recovery groups and communities in which individuals feel welcomed and accepted is essential in promoting and supporting this form of identity change.

However, within the connections model, identity is not a sufficient change. As we have demonstrated in our work in the UK (Best et al, 2011) and in the US (Cano et al, 2017), the benefits of changes in social networks are significantly enhanced by engagement in meaningful activities. In the Florida project with recovery residences, for instance, it was engagement in a range of meaningful activities that significantly enhanced the value of retention in the programme, leading to improvements in both personal and social recovery capital and from that to increased wellbeing. This is part of a process of increased active participation in activities and groups, that will both create a sense of purpose and meaning and increase the bind to the groups. As with our understanding of mutual aid groups, where active participation is a much better predictor of outcomes than attendance, we would assume that engaging in groups that require active participation and action will result in markedly more positive outcomes. Further, active participation in groups further binds the changes in identity (personal and social) and creates new networks (social capital) that affords better access to things that are available in the local area through these new connections (community capital).

And so the final piece of the CHIME jigsaw is around empowerment. Within a social identity model of change, this involves a virtuous circle of social engagement, purposeful action and an increased sense of wellbeing manifest in a growing sense of self-esteem and self-efficacy. In the approach to CHIME derived from the data presented in this book, the growth of personal recovery capital is captured in the empowerment component in which the individual derives personal strengths (and awareness of those strengths) from this cycle of positive identity change, engagement in meaningful and pro-social activity, and increased empowerment and self-determination. But there is also a cyclical quality to the whole thing with that improvement in self-efficacy and empowerment also supporting and sustaining growth in connections and continuing to fuel the sense of hope and belief in personal and in collective recovery.

In sum, effective linkage generates a sense of hope and belief that change is possible. It is this that creates both the motivation and the conditions that allow the positive dynamic generation of personal growth and positive social identities and acceptance. This theme will be explored further in the following section.

Hope and meaning

The question that will be addressed in this section is about the role that hope plays in the model outlined, and how it can permeate not only each phase of this personal journey but also have a positive impact on those in contact with hope-based connections, as is shown in Figure 8.1.

The key point here is that hope is generative and that not only does it benefit the person in recovery, there is also a residual effect that ripples out in the short and longer term. This has been a major theme for this work and is really around the idea that recovery spreads not only through vulnerable populations but by disseminating hope and connection across a much wider range of groups and communities. This is the key idea from Braithwaite (2013) that social capital is not something that diminishes when it is drawn upon but conversely that the more it is used, the more it grows. In the family connector programme at HMP Kirkham, this was evident not only in the engagement

Figure 8.1: CHIME, hope and reciprocal growth

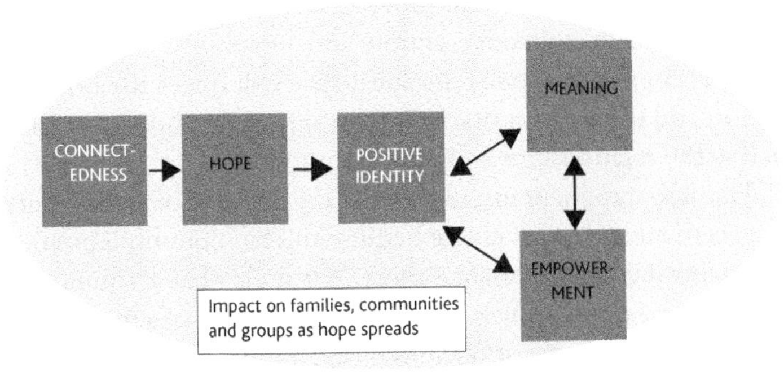

and enthusiasm of the prisoners and the family members, but also more surprisingly in the enthusiasm and invigoration of the probation staff who participated in the project. There was also a wider effect with other prison staff coming to view sessions because they had heard about the positive experience and the sense of collective purpose and they wanted to see it for themselves.

For all three of these stakeholder groups, the elevated sense of hope and wellbeing was experienced in three ways: internally, as dyadic relationships, and in terms of the group. In other words, there was a growth in personal wellbeing, an improvement in interpersonal relationships and a commitment to the group as an emerging base for social and community capital. Yet, the impact is experienced well beyond those three groups and is felt more widely in the community.

This is a generative process in which community capital grows as a result of the process, enriching life within and beyond the group in the prison, through the increases in the radius of trust (Fukuyama, 2001), and potentially into the community through the endeavours of the staff and the family members effectively engaging community groups. This social contagion relies on the links being in place to allow spread to happen beyond the recovery community and to impact on a broad range of groups, excluded and included. However, underpinning the growth in interpersonal trust and the commitment to the group was a sense of hope around shared values of successful desistance, recovery and reintegration back into the community. Of course, this is not a simple process or a straight road, but it is an antidote to apathy and indifference that provides motivation and inspiration and a belief in collective action and possibility. What hope provides in this process is the spirit that will direct the body to action and the oxygen that will then spread that hope and trust across the relationships and communities.

This is so important in a model that is predicated on community engagement and social justice because this has not only a positive effect on the capital balance sheet, but it also has a cumulative one for recovery resources. This is where the idea of a therapeutic landscape fits into the model (Wilton and DeVerteuil, 2006), in that place is a key domain for assessing change and monitoring the growth of wellbeing. The crucial aim of creating diverse and accessible pathways from recovery groups into a range of community resources is to ensure the viability and accessibility of those pathways for future groups of people seeking recovery. The positive sum of this game is that hope is contagious and so as the path is trodden more frequently, so the belief in its impact grows and its salience and accessibility also grow.

This links to the role of meaningful activities and a sense of purpose. One of the most striking and important lessons from JFH was the pride the apprentices took in doing something that made a difference and that contributed to their mates, to the organisation and also to the local community, where they started to feel a sense of pride and a sense that they belonged. The impact of meaningful activities on wellbeing has been articulated above but in part this results from a growing sense of self-esteem, self-efficacy and pride that results from participation and achievement, and that helps to overcome self-stigma and the internalisation of negative labels.

However, there is a strong association between meaningful activities and connections that results from shared activities and shared goals that help to build collective efficacy and a positive self-identity. This is part of the reason that the connectors group become a bonded and cohesive group – there is a sense of collective efficacy that is suffused with shared purpose and burgeoning hope.

One of the most exciting things about the Kirkham Family Connectors programme was the recognition that this can arise in the context of the prison and across the perceived adversarial boundaries between the prisoners and the prison staff. Admittedly, Kirkham is a Category D prison for those within two years of release, and the programme has yet to be tested in other prison types, but this is an important discovery for this body of work and suggests that the process may help to build positive relationships. As previously stated, the process of asset mapping and training connectors generates at least as much benefit as the outcome. This sense of belonging is contingent on there being successes and achievements for the group and the building of collective efficacy and blossoming hope that results from every success.

Community engagement and social justice

This is not exclusively a question of bonding capital within the group, but also about linking and bridging capital (Putnam and Feldstein, 2004). The success of the process relies not only on successful bonds occurring within the group, but also on the ability of the group to effectively engage with a range of diverse resources in the local community, and for those groups to engage actively and openly with the recovery or desistance groups. This is the major challenge around strategic leadership in promoting active social justice, and the importance of achieving successes that are visible and identifiable beyond the recovery group or community.

What happened in the Sheffield Community Connectors project in Sheffield was driven by inspirational leaders, as was the case in the Magistrates Court in Dandenong, in the Salvation Army Recovery Centres on the Gold Coast and in a number of the UK locations described in the book. In virtually all of these settings, however, it has been a representative of the vulnerable population who has been the driving force and has actively engaged external stakeholders, either someone in long-term recovery or someone who is relatively early in their own journey. They have effectively reached out to external community groups and worked with their own teams and clients to actively engage resources that exist in the community. What is unique about the recovery cities idea is that the civic organisations that represent some of those community resources will actively take on that role. What changes with this model is two things – the first, an attempt not just to teach by example but also to create a community model that builds inclusion and social justice and, second, strategic direction – as outlined in the ROSC work by Sheedy and Whitter (2009). The ultimate aim in this model is to increase the overall pool of social capital in a community to increase what Sampson and Laub (2003) would have referred to as social cohesion and which we refer to as social capital. This is the strength and inter-connectedness of bonds across communities with as many bridges and links as possible between 'nodes', whether the nodes refer to isolated individuals or ostracised and excluded social groups. Community engagement is a process of building connections and hope that challenges exclusion and changes communities to allow them to support recovery and desistance pathways.

Visible recovery and social identity

This notion of integrated approaches to recovery and desistance are linked to the idea that recovery as a movement needs to have an accessible and visible component. As I outlined in a paper with colleagues from Australia (Beckwith et al, 2016), recovery has come to be seen as a social movement (in the paper we describe it as a 'pre-figurative' political movement, to capture the sense of a group with an emerging consciousness of its own influence and collective capability). This adds to our understanding and our definitions of recovery – and what may be lacking around desistance – the sense that recovery is something to belong to and to be proud of being a part of. This is most evident in the annual recovery walks that take place in the UK and which SARRG has organised and managed in Sheffield, and Aspire achieves with its Recovery Games. People come together to celebrate recovery and to have fun, but also to share that sense of achievement and pride with others, only some of whom will be in recovery. The key point from a social contagion perspective is that the more visible, accessible and attractive a recovery group is, the more likely people with addictions problems are to aspire to join and to fulfil that aspiration.

Haslam et al (2018: 17) have argued that

> In the most basic sense, groups make life worth living, and they are what we live for … By the same token if groups exert a negative influence on our lives (as they sometimes do) or if we lack or lose valuable group memberships, then we can see that social identity processes will be implicated in poor health outcomes.

This was the foundation for our own SIMOR in 2016 – that most recidivistic offenders and substance misusers lack positive social supports and group memberships through the disruptions to family life and through exclusion and stigmatisation brought about by their lifestyles. Thus, the challenge is to support the transition from negative group membership (with its adverse impact on health) to positive groups that can confer the wellbeing benefits that Cath Haslam and her colleagues describe.

This is precisely what is illustrated by Café Sobar as a hub for recovery. While physically, it provides a positive space for social engagement and interaction, it also affords opportunities for new group engagements associated with recovery, community and education, and that allows people to remove themselves from risky behaviours and groups in doing so. In the SIMOR (Best et al, 2016), the challenge is around motivating and inspiring people to move from using to recovery groups and it is here that visibility and attractiveness of a recovery community is important, and that it is seen as accessible and available, not only to those seeking to recover for the first time but also to those who have slips and relapses in their recovery journey. This is where both recovery champions and navigators, and more broadly an inclusive and supportive community, act to support that process of attraction and engagement.

Recovery as a social movement

While the summary of UK recovery initiatives collected with Jeffrey Roth (Roth and Best, 2013) summarised visible recovery initiatives in the UK including the emerging UK annual recovery walk, the start of recovery activities (such as the recovery walking group in North Wales) and recovery cafes (such as the Serenity Café in Edinburgh), the importance of recovery as a social movement was not fully recognised at that point.

What Melinda Beckwith's paper on recovery as a form of pre-figurative politics (Beckwith et al, 2016) has added to this discussion, and what we have referred to earlier in this chapter and in previous chapters, is a sense of how important the growth of a visible collective movement is to many people both new to recovery and established in their recovery journeys. This is social identity in action – what matters most is that sense of belonging to something that is attractive and engaging and that has high status and value. According to Haslam et al (2018: 46), 'The status of those groups [to which we belong] not only affects the self-esteem and wellbeing we derive as a group member (e.g. collective self-esteem …) but also our personal self-esteem and wellbeing (Jetten et al, 2015)'.

For people in recovery in the UK (and the US) there is a twin sense of belonging that is available – to the individual groups they belong to, and also the sense that they belong to a social movement that has status and impact at a national and at an international level. As the walks and events proliferate and succeed, so that sense of collective efficacy can grow through visible recovery communities in a way that is not possible for anonymous fellowships (although there is nothing incompatible about the two things). The key point from Haslam et al (2018) is that this filters down to create personal wellbeing and a sense of belonging and empowerment. In this way, the CHIME process has a form of contagion that is collective as well as personal. This can happen at a macro level as with a national movement but it has also happened at a local level as illustrated by the case studies of JFH and Café Sobar. In both these cases, there are opportunities to celebrate recovery success, to be embedded in communities of recovery and in social groups that create strong binds around recovery successes and wellbeing (as outlined by Moos, 2007). In both of these cases, there was a strong sense of pride and commitment to the organisations linked to bonding capital, and a sense of dynamism, energy and success that people want to be a part of. This was best evidenced in the SNA carried out on the JFH Facebook page where retention (and so outcomes) are best predicted by being central in the social network, being widely endorsed by other members and using language that expresses collective commitment. This is consistent with the evidence about AA (Kaskutas et al, 2009; Kelly and Yeterian, 2008) which suggests that attendance at mutual aid meetings confers only a small benefit but that active engagement in groups creates a much stronger bind.

This is consistent with the social identity model already outlined, but here the crucial point is that the hope for recovery can be inspired by active engagement in a social movement promoting change and challenging stigma and exclusion. As has been argued in the context of immigrant groups (Jasinskaja-Lahti et al, 2006), individuals are more likely to be able to cope with exclusion when they band together in a group that affords them a positive identity and that can challenge the exclusions and discriminations that stigma can bring. The recovery movement has an identity that exists beyond the individuals in recovery or even the groups they belong to and suggests a collective mission and goal and a sense of energy that transcends specific philosophies and approaches and characterises recovery as something that is dynamic, positive, collective and inclusive.

The role of the professional and the practitioner: recovery coalitions

This does not mean, however, that there is not a role for professionals or practitioners in supporting and actively encouraging recovery supports and pathways. Much of the focus of this book – from the early work with the Salvation Army and the Magistrates Court in Dandenong – has focused on the role of professionals both as strategic leaders in an inclusive approach to community connections and as active participants in the delivery of this model. This is often easier said than done but a recovery-oriented and inclusive culture is a strong magnet and attraction for encouraging professionals and peers to work together and to do so in more than an ad hoc manner, underpinned by a clear strategic direction.

While recovery-oriented capacity building relies on peer activities and the championing of peer mentors and navigators, the fundamental premise is that there needs to be a coalition of professionals and peers, along with family members and other representatives of the wider community to ensure that there is maximised access to community resources (through a range of personal networks) and a sharing of learning and skills. This is to ensure that there is both a greater coverage of communities and access to a wider range of community assets.

From the initial Australian studies, the principles of a recovery-oriented system of care articulated by Kelly and White (2011) were evidenced in the work of the magistrates in Dandenong and the managers at the Salvation Army who recognised that they needed to focus on community engagement, strengths-based approaches and continuity of care and support for people attempting to sustain recovery and desistance pathways.

However, this was not done as a form of 'cold' referral where clients were given contact details and told to get on with things. The fundamental aim was around assertive linkage and engagement with peers and professionals central to the approach of not only initial connection but also the broader goals of maintaining relationships and active engagement. This is also critical to the generative part of the project and the creation of new community resources and community connections. There are many examples from the projects outlined in the book, but the two that are worth commenting on are the Kirkham Family Connectors and the Sheffield Community Connectors programme.

In Kirkham, the shared sense of vision and enterprise contributed significantly to the success of the project and the underlying growth of group bonding and trust. What emerged was a clear example of what Fukuyama (2001) referred to as a 'radius of trust' in which the contagion of hope generated by the strengths-based activities created a positive energy and a shared sense of belonging and achievement across the three groups who were involved. As Snyder (2000) has argued, hopeful thinkers are more able to achieve their goals than people who feel hopeless, and there is evidence that hope is linked to recovery from a range of illnesses (Good et al, 1990). While one unanticipated good that came out of the Kirkham project was the strengthening of relationships between prisoners and family members, an even more unexpected benefit was the inclusion of the probation staff in this hope-based model. To a large degree, this resulted from their openness and active engagement and the extent to which they actively participated in the programme as equals of the prisoners and the family members.

A similar relationship emerged in the Community Connectors work in Sheffield, where senior managers from a range of participating organisations took an active role in the project. This was essential not only to show leadership within the group but also to enact those principles of a recovery-oriented system that involve strategic vision combined with grassroots activity. However, it is also critical in engaging a range of frontline staff in recovery groups and activities and in creating linking capital across key areas of the recovery coalition, based on shared objectives and positive strategic values. This has been critical in addressing the key points outlined by Kelly and White (2011) in their ideas of creating recovery-oriented systems that have accessible and equable treatment systems embedded in recovery communities that are holistic and multi-faceted to support individual choices and evolving and emerging needs. Fundamentally, this is a model that creates the conditions that supports and permits pathways to lasting change but that grows and benefits in response to those changes. In the next section we move on to the role that recovery plays in understanding both the personal pathway and how it can be integrated with the CHIME In Action.

What is recovery capital?

In the original model of recovery capital, Granfield and Cloud (2001) coined the term 'recovery capital', defined as 'the sum total of one's resources that can be brought to bear on the initiation and maintenance of substance misuse cessation' (Cloud and Granfield, 2009: 1972). There are four components of recovery capital that they discussed in their original model. These are: social capital, referring to the amount of supportive relationships an individual may have; physical capital, referring to tangible items such as property and money; human capital, referring to an individual's aspirations, skills and positive health; and cultural capital, which is made up from a person's beliefs, values and attitudes which link to social conformity (Cloud and Granfield, 2009). However, in the 2009 paper, Cloud and Granfield introduced the concept of negative recovery capital to deal with barriers to recovery based on the idea that certain life experiences (ongoing mental health problems, criminal justice histories) and certain demographic factors (age and gender) influenced the likelihood of lasting recovery.

In Best and Laudet's (2010) paper reviewing the structure of recovery capital, it was divided into three categories – personal, social and community – and the latter was critical in terms of contextual factors that shaped recovery pathways. In our view, it is the dynamic interaction with the community, and the extent to which it can be seen as a therapeutic landscape, that establishes the ground on which the recovery road is built both for individuals and for groups.

This became the foundation for subsequent work on attempting to operationalise recovery capital in two separate measures: the Assessment of Recovery Capital (Groshkova et al, 2012), measuring personal and social capital; and the Recovery Group Participation Scale (Groshkova et al, 2011), to measure active participation in community recovery groups. The aim was to start to operationalise recovery capital so that it could be measured consistently and reliably and that over time change could be detected. This knowledge could then be used to support recovery champions and navigators and to allow people in recovery some sense of where they were and what they still needed to do in their recovery journey.

Our subsequent work on the REC-CAP (Cano et al, 2017) has gone one step further in linking an overall profile of recovery resources and strengths, with a section on barriers to recovery and unmet support needs, to inform recovery care planning. What is behind this idea is that recovery is something that grows over time but that this will not be linear nor will it be consistent across all domains. Moreover, recovery capital can be measured, and can change over time, and crucially this change can be planned and supported through peer champions and through active community engagement.

Therefore, there is a need for a process of monitoring and measuring recovery in coherent and consistent ways. Our REC-CAP system is based on the idea that recovery is a gradual process that will generally require partnership and the active engagement of assets in the local community, and that both internal motivation and external support can assist this process. The REC-CAP model is also strengths-based in two senses – strengths can form the primary route to recovery (as opposed to attempting to minimise illness or pathology factors), and existing strengths and resources (personal, social and community) can be used to achieve the goals that the person aspires to.

The underpinning model of the REC-CAP model (Cano et al, 2017; Best and DeAlwis, 2017) is that there are three cyclical stages to supporting recovery based on building recovery models: Measure, Plan and Engage. In this model, the recovery care planning session identifies existing recovery capital in the three domains (as well as barriers to recovery and unmet needs), and how they have changed since the last session, which would typically have been around three months earlier. The year is then divided up into four equal periods, each of which allows a sufficient window to make meaningful changes and to create a plan. If progress is good, this frequency can reduce, but for the first few years, quarterly sessions allow opportunities for review, for planning and for consolidating success. The completion of the assessment informs the initial stage of a recovery care (the Plan) stage that reviews successes achieved in the previous quarter and informs the development of plans that are built on strengths and resources, for the next quarter. The final component is Engage, as the model assumes that effective engagement with community resources is an essential part of ongoing resources.

This is in part a consequence of the need for recovery to be an active process that involves doing. But it is also because, for the vast majority of people starting a recovery journey, they will not have sufficient internal or personal resources, nor sufficient pro-social group memberships, to enable and support their recovery pathway.

In the model that we tested with recovery residences in Florida (Cano et al, 2017), it was peer recovery navigators who acted as the partners or confederates of the person in recovery and there is no assumption that the navigator has to be a professional with a particular set of qualifications. They do need to be able to generate a strong and trusting relationship, and the sense of hope and belief in the person and in their relationship. From this will spring the external contacts and partnerships that are the second core part of the navigator's role. They are responsible for taking on the role of community connector, by being the bridge between the individual in recovery and the assets in the community. For this, they need to be aware of the assets that are out there and where possible be able to create effective connections and linkages, preparing and supporting the person to engage and providing them with the support they need to make the most of the groups and resources they engage with.

This is at the heart of the CHIME In Action model where the role of the navigator or champion is about supporting effective engagement with recovery groups and communities. The peer equivalent of a therapeutic alliance is the start of a radius of trust which can inspire the drive and motivation that will enable the transition into the cycle of meaningful activities, linked to a sense of empowerment and self-esteem that will inform the development of a new set of social identities linked to positive groups and activities. The enactment of the 'helper principle' here is that this will also promote and support a similar dynamic in the peer navigator. And it is from this relationship that the grey circle in Figure 8.1 starts to emerge. This is the added value of relational models, in that they not only create virtuous circles in the progression of the individual at the centre of the model, they also radiate out generating, first, a positive alliance and, second, benefits that impact on families and communities. Figure 8.2 shows how this manifests itself in terms of the idea of recovery (or desistance) capital.

The white box at the bottom of the figure illustrates how this then influences the wider community. The ultimate aim is that the grey zone increases in its community cohesion – driven by improved connections and increased levels of hope – but also that this contagion expands both geographically and into new connections, groups and communities. This is an intrinsically ecological model of capital in which community recovery capital is a dynamic force that will grow as inclusion and opportunity increase and will diminish where stigma, exclusion and disintegrative shaming come to dominate local communities.

Figure 8.2: CHIME, capital and reciprocal growth

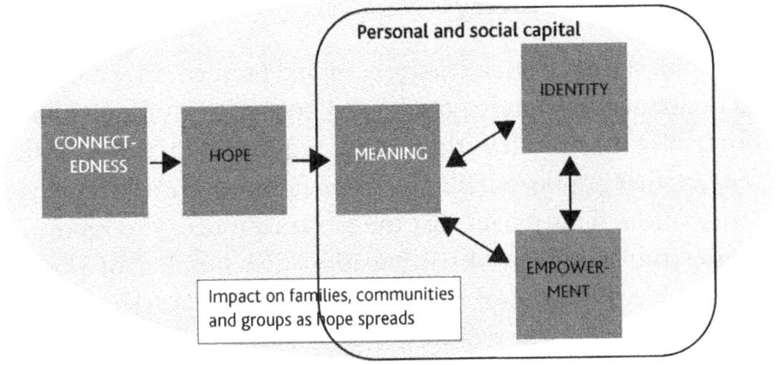

The model is about individual pathways to recovery as they are embedded in groups and communities, but the impact of each successful journey is experienced and has ramifications for the community itself, which is not seen as immutable in this process. As recovery growth happens in groups it impacts on the perceptions of the possibility of recovery and on the beliefs about connection and about engagement in the community itself.

In this CHIME In Action approach, building a therapeutic landscape for recovery (Wilton and DeVerteuil, 2006) is essentially a process of building effective and successful communities in which trust and social cohesion are built on effective connection and the mobilisation of strengths and resources in a community. This occurs through a process of social contagion and connection with hope and inclusion as the primary things that are transmitted and sustained. In this model, recovery capital is not seen as exclusively a property of individuals but an evolving community resource in which there must be a constant striving for inclusion and active participation. Yet, as with the individual pathway, this is not something that is easy to achieve, and requires commitment by a large number of stakeholders and our work on recovery and inclusive cities is part of the attempt to address some of these challenges around citizenship and inclusion. It is also something that can easily be lost without ongoing commitment and support. The level of inclusion and hope is a fluid concept that will change over time. The next section will examine the implications of the CHIME In Action model for policy and practice in more depth.

The role of policy and societal responses: tertiary desistance and recovery

This book started from a relatively simple premise, that recovery and desistance will rarely be achieved on the back of individuals' efforts alone, and that there is a requirement for a social contract that supports effective reintegration and active civic participation. This means that the personal journey to recovery requires the support and participation of a number of people that include, but are not restricted to, family and friends. This may also include peer workers, mutual aid group members and sponsors, but also wider 'structural' factors and frameworks. These include potential employers, admissions workers at college and university, probation officers, housing workers and for each of them the myriad of rules they are obliged to comply with. Yet all of these people are also members of the community and their responses are likely to be shaped by the attitudes, experiences and values that pervade in the community. In this context, visible and accessible recovery will help to shift and build positive community capital and increase both hope and openness to inclusive attitudes.

To support this, there needs to be strong leadership at a local and national level around citizenship and inclusion. While drug addiction is the most stigmatised health condition and alcohol the fourth most stigmatised (World Health Organization, 2001), there is a huge risk that individuals become labelled and marginalised, and are not allowed to be reintegrated back into their communities when they are undertaking their recovery journeys. In 2013, Phillips and Shaw reported on the findings of an online survey of the general public who were asked a range of questions about social distance. What this means is that participants were asked about how willing they would be to have various people live next door to them, for instance, or look after their children. The key finding of the study was that not only were people less keen to have addicts living next door to them or dating their sisters than obese people or smokers, the same applied to people in recovery. The survey respondents only made a slight distinction between people who had active addictions and those they were told were in recovery, suggesting that in the minds of the general public recovery is not real or not without risk. When this is translated to day-to-day activities, it has profound ramifications for what Maruna and Farrall (2004) referred to as tertiary desistance in the context of overcoming crime careers. If the public (and professionals) continue to discriminate against those who have made substantial attempts to recover or desist, then many will ultimately fail based on lack of opportunity and a failure to establish the basic life foundations of reasonable housing, a job that confers respect and dignity, and access to the resources that are available in the local community. In other words, experts in criminology have reached the same conclusion about rehabilitation – for it to be fully achieved requires not only social group changes but also effective societal responses that promote inclusion and engagement.

This is where there is a clear need for leadership – and where a recovery-oriented system of care (Kelly and White, 2011; Sheedy and Whitter, 2009) will fail if it does not address wider societal concerns. In Kelly and White's (2011) edited book on addiction recovery management, they discuss a number of case studies of successfully established recovery communities that afford opportunity and access and this is what will be needed on a much larger scale. The reason for our inclusive recovery cities model is a recognition of the fact that recovery goes way beyond treatment and even its partner organisations. What limited evidence exists in this area is largely American and this model needs to be expanded considerably into the UK and in other parts of the world and used to develop an evidence base about what works at a community level.

For policy makers, this means that there can be no platitudes about 'joined up working' or 'cradle to grave' care as the models should not be reliant exclusively on a range of professionals without community input, and without a recognition of the unique resources and assets that exist in each community. Nor should the pendulum swing so far to the other end that professionals can abnegate their responsibilities and leave all of the navigation and coordination to peers and volunteers. The point of a coalition can best be conceptualised within a model of bonding, linking and bridging social capital. A coalition of community connectors, professionals, peers and families affords access to a diverse range of resources and capabilities, and this is what strategic leaders and policy makers should be aspiring to.

An effective coalition will reinforce existing networks and invigorate them with the aim and goal of inclusion, will lead to stronger links within existing networks but crucially will lead to bridges between previously unconnected individuals and groups. It is from this that the social contagion of hope can emerge. While individuals will come and go from the groups, if the message is strong and clear enough, and there are sufficient grassroots, professional and strategic leaders with commitment to the process, then spread of the model and the message will be achieved. Additionally, as has been pointed out previously, the coalition that is involved in identifying community assets, engaging and training connectors and then mobilising the assets, itself emerges as a new form of asset in the community.

As was illustrated in the context of the Kirkham Family Connectors programme, building alliances and coalitions based on hope and strengths with a relational focus, a community embedding and a forward vision generates wellbeing that is experienced both internally and interpersonally and so builds a positive sense of social identity and group engagement and commitment. There are, therefore, two forms of positive contagion: the first is through the creation of new community assets built on hope that is a part of the connections process – and which local policy makers and strategic leaders should aspire to do; and the second is through contagion via the networks of all of those actively involved in the process of community building. This invigorated existing relationships (between prisoners and their family members) and created new relationships (between members of different families) and all with a ripple effect that influenced officers and the wider prison environment.

This is ABCD in action. The increased UK focus on this model as a core part of a recovery system is entirely consistent with the idea of mobilising communities to support vulnerable populations to access community resources and so build social and community capital. What policy makers and decision makers can add to this is twofold: first, they can use their own connections and influence to mobilise community assets and to provide resources where this is possible and appropriate. Second, they are in a position to nurture and support the 'bigger picture' by actively promoting community and professional involvement in the process of positive contagion and connection rather than relying on NGOs and community groups to support the process. Finally, they have a core role in helping to remove structural and attitudinal barriers to effective reintegration.

What we are hoping to achieve with the inclusive cities work that is currently ongoing (Best and Colman, 2018), and is engaging a number of UK and European cities, is a commitment to integration and reintegration and a celebration of innovation. We already know that the cities that are participating – like many others – have incredible examples of civic society and dynamic partnerships between communities and state-run organisations, and our task is to identify the effective elements, assess their transferability and attempt to codify underlying principles of strengths-based partnership working. In essence, we are not asking policy makers to do anything other than build communities through connectedness and hope, and to champion the successes and innovations they already achieve. This is an attempt to celebrate collective commitment to recovery and to create a learning culture and a shared set of values and aspirations from that model to build inclusive and rehabilitative cities.

So what now?

There are no geographic boundaries to this work and this closing section focuses on work I am doing in both the UK and the US to bridge together the ideas of recovery capital, CHIME In Action and Connected Communities, in both community and prison contexts. The two projects are linked and they are an attempt to advance the ideas put forward in this book in a systematic approach to recovery navigation outlined in the acronym MPE:

- **M**easure
- **P**lan
- **E**ngage

This model involves providing a systematic mapping of recovery strengths and resources, and using these to develop a recovery plan that is operationalised through active engagement with a range of community supports or resources. This model is designed to bring to reality a relational and strengths-based approach to recovery interventions and support.

Cano et al (2017), looking at the Florida partnership, showed the added value of engaging in meaningful activities to support ongoing recovery and to add value to retention in recovery residences. This work was done in partnership with the Florida Association of Recovery Residences (FARR) and eight residences, who provided a cohort of recovery navigators to work with clients to deliver the assessment and help to shape and implement the resulting recovery care plan, based on a quarterly cycle of activity.

What sits behind this approach is a software system that means the recovery navigator sits and completes the REC-CAP measure (which takes around 15 minutes) on a laptop or even on a phone, and this is immediately translated into a visual depiction of the scores. There is no data input and there is no need for delay – and this is what makes it possible for the assessment to be used immediately to inform the recovery care planning process. However, it is not an automated process (Best and DeAlwis, 2017), with the recovery care plan partly informed by the score profile on the questionnaires and partly by the client's own experiences and views and needs. This means that the recovery navigator and the client jointly negotiate and own the resulting care plan which is based on the principles of node-link mapping (Dansereau and Simpson, 2009), to ensure a shared visualisation of the resulting product. This is the next stage in evidencing a recovery journey that takes time and commitment, the commitment of the person in recovery, their family and friends, but also the wider community. When this journey happens, all of those groups will benefit as there will be a contagion of hope and a commitment to inclusion and collective wellbeing. I hope you too will commit to supporting this process.

References

ACT Law Reform Advisory Council (2017) *Canberra – Becoming a Restorative City: Progress Report on Community Ideas from Preliminary Conclusions*. Reference 5: ACT Government.

Adler, P. (2002) 'Social capital: Prospects for a new concept', *Academy of Management Review*, 27(1): 17–40.

Andrews, D. and Bonta, J. (1998) *The Psychology of Criminal Conduct* (2nd edition), Cincinnati, OH: Anderson.

Australian Bureau of Statistics (2013) '2011 Census Quick Stats: Greater Dandenong', www.censusdata.abs.gov.au/census_services/getproduct/census/2011/quickstat/LGA22670

Beckwith, M., Best, D. and Bliuc, A. (2016) 'What the recovery movement tells us about pre-figurative politics', *Journal of Social and Political Psychology*, 4(1): 238–51.

Best, D. (2014) *Strength, Support, Setbacks and Solutions: The developmental pathway to addiction recovery*, Brighton: Pavilion Publishing.

Best, D. (2015) *The Australian Life in Recovery Survey*, Melbourne, Australia: Turning Point, Eastern Health.

Best, D. (2016) 'An unlikely hero?' *Drug and Alcohol Today*, 16(1): 106–16.

Best, D. and Colman, C. (2018) 'Let's celebrate recovery. Inclusive cities working together to support social cohesion', *Addiction Research and Theory*, doi: 10.1080/16066359.2018.1520223

Best, D. and DeAlwis, S. (2017) 'Community recovery as a public health intervention: The contagion of hope', *Alcoholism Treatment Quarterly*, doi: 10.1080/07347324.2017.1318647

Best, D. and Laudet, A. (2010) *The Potential of Recovery Capital*, London: RSA.

Best, D., Savic, M. and Daley, P. (2016) 'The wellbeing of alcohol and other drug counsellors in Australia: strengths, risks and implications', *Alcoholism Treatment Quarterly*, 34(2): 223–32.

Best, D., Bliuc, A., Iqbal, M., Upton, K. & Hodgkins, S. (2018) 'Mapping social identity change in online networks of addiction recovery', *Addiction Research and Theory*, 26 (3): 163–173.

Best, D., Ghufran, S., Day, E., Ray, R. and Loaring, J. (2008) 'Breaking the habit: A retrospective analysis of desistance factors among formerly problematic heroin users', *Drug and Alcohol Review*, 27(6): 619–24.

Best, D., Gow, J., Taylor, A., Knox, A. & White, W. (2011) 'Recovery from heroin or alcohol dependence: A qualitative account of the recovery experience in Glasgow', *Journal of Drug Issues*, 11 (1): 359–378.

Best, D., Loudon, L., Powell, D., Groshkova, T. and White, W. (2013) 'Identifying and recruiting recovery champions: Exploratory action research in Barnsley, South Yorkshire', *Journal of Groups in Addiction and Recovery*, 8(3): 169–84.

Best, D., Byrne, G., Pullen, D., Kelly, J., Elliot, K. and Savic, M. (2014a) 'Therapeutic communities and the local community: Isolation or integration', *Therapeutic Communities Journal*, 35(4): 150–8.

Best, D., Lubman, D., Savic, M., Wilson, A., Dingle, G., Haslam, A., Haslam, C. and Jetten, J. (2014b) 'Social identity and transitional identity: Exploring social networks and their significance in a therapeutic community setting', *Therapeutic Community Journal*, 35(1): 10–20.

Best, D., Albertson, K., Irving, J., Lightowlers, C., Mama-Rudd, A. and Chaggar, A. (2015a) *The UK Life in Recovery Survey 2015: The First National UK Survey of Addiction RECOVERY experiences*, Sheffield: Helena Kennedy Centre for International Justice, Sheffield Hallam University.

Best, D., Beckwith, M., Haslam, C., Haslam, S.A., Jetten, J., Mawson, E. and Lubman, D.I. (2015b) 'Overcoming alcohol and other drug addiction as a process of social identity transition: The Social Identity Model of Recovery (SIMOR)', *Addiction Research & Theory*, 24(2): 1–13, doi: 10.3109/16066359.2015.1075980

Best, D., Rome, A., Hanning, K., White, W., Gossop, M., Taylor, A. & Perkins, A. (2015c) 'Research for recovery: A review of the drugs evidence base', *Crime and Justice Social Research*, Scottish Government: Edinburgh.

Betty Ford Institute Consensus Group (2007) 'What is recovery? A working definition from the Betty Ford Institute', *Journal of Substance Abuse Treatment*, 33: 221–8.

Biernacki, P. (1986) *Pathways from Heroin Addiction: Recovery without Treatment*, Philadelphia: Temple University Press.

Bliuc, A-M., Best, D., Iqbal, M. and Upton, K. (2017) 'Building addiction recovery capital through online participation in a recovery community', *Social Science and Medicine*, 193: 110–17.

Boman, J. and Mowen, T. (2017) 'Building the ties that bind, breaking the ties that don't: Family support, criminal peers and reentry success', *Criminology and Public Policy*, 16(3): 753–73.

Bourdieu, P. (1985) 'The forms of capital', in J.G. Richardson (ed), *Handbook of Theory and Research for the Sociology of Education*, New York: Greenwood.

Braithwaite, J. (2013) 'Relational republican regulation', *Regulation and Governance*, 7(1): 124–144.

Brunton-Smith, I. and McCarthy, D. (2017) 'The Effects of Prisoner Attachment to Family on Re-entry Outcomes: A Longitudinal Assessment', *The British Journal of Criminology*, 57(2): 463–482.

Butler, M., Savic, M., Best, D., Manning, V., Mills, K. and Lubman, D. (2018) 'Wellbeing and coping strategies of alcohol and other drug therapeutic community workers: a qualitative study', *Therapeutic Communities: The International Journal of Therapeutic Communities*, 39(3): 118–28.

Cano, I., Best, D., Edwards, M. and Lehman, J. (2017) 'Recovery capital pathways: Mapping the components of recovery wellbeing', *Drug and Alcohol Dependence*, 181: 11–19.

Christakis, N. and Fowler, J. (2009) *Connected: The Amazing Power of Social Networks and How They Shape Our Lives*, New York: Little Brown.

Chung, C.K. and Pennebaker, J.W. (2014) 'Counting little words in big data: The psychology of communities, culture, and history', in J. P. Forgas, O. Vincze, & J. László (eds), *Social Cognition and Communication*, New York: Psychology Press, pp 25–42.

Clinks and Social Firms UK (2014) *Providing Employment and Training Opportunities for Offenders. Growing Sustainable Work Integration Social Enterprises. A Report of Learning from this Programme*, www.gov.uk/government/uploads/system/uploads/attachment_data/file/305974/Providing_employment_training_opportunities_for_offenders.pdf

Cloud, W. and Granfield, R. (2008) 'Conceptualising recovery capital: Expansion of a theoretical construct', *Substance Use and Misuse*, 43(12–13): 1971–86.

Codd, H. (2007) 'Prisoners' families and resettlement: a critical analysis', *Howard Journal*, 46: 255–63.

Coleman, J. (1988) 'Social capital in the creation of human capital', *The American Journal of Sociology*, 94: S95–S120.

Comfort, M. (2003) Home sweep: the social and cultural consequences of mass imprisonment for women with imprisoned partners, unpublished PhD thesis, University of London.

Community Indicators Victoria (2013) *Greater Dandenong Wellbeing Report*, Community Indicators Victoria, www.communityindicators.net.au/wellbeing_reports/greater_dandenong

Cruwys, T., Haslam, S.A., Dingle, G.A., Haslam, C. and Jetten, J. (2014) 'Depression and social identity: An integrative review', *Personality and Social Psychology Review*, 18(3): 215–38, doi: 10.1177/1088868314523839

Czuchry, M. and Dansereau, D.F. (2003) 'A model of the effects of node-link mapping on drug abuse counseling', *Addictive Behaviors*, 28(3): 537–49.

Dansereau, D.F. and Simpson, D.D. (2009) 'A picture is worth a thousand words: The case for graphic representations', *Professional Psychology: Research & Practice*, 40(1): 104–10.

DeLeon, G. (2000) *Community as Method. Theory, Model and Method*, Springer: New York.

Dennis, M., Scott, C. and Laudet, A. (2014) 'Beyond bricks and mortars: recent research on substance abuse disorder recovery management', *Current Psychiatry Report*, 1–7.

De Silva, M., McKenzie, M., Harpham, T. and Huttly, S. (2005) 'Social capital and mental illness: A systematic review', *Journal of Epidemiology and Community Health*, 59: 619–27.

Dingle, G.A., Brander, C., Ballantyne, J. and Baker, F.A. (2012) '"To be heard": The social and mental health benefits of choir singing for disadvantaged adults', *Psychology of Music*, 41(4): 405–21.

Duwe, G. and Clark, V. (2012) 'The importance of social support for prisoner reentry: the effects of visitation on offender recidivism', *Correction Today*, 74(2): 46–50.

Farmer, Lord (2017) *The Importance of Strengthening Prisoners' Family Ties to Prevent Reoffending and Reduce Intergenerational Crime*, London: Ministry of Justice.

Farrall, S. (2002) *Rethinking What Works with Offenders: Probation, Social Context and Desistance from Crime*, Devon: Willan Publishing.

Flora, C. and Flora, J. (2013) *Rural communities: Legacy and change* (4th edition), Boulder, CO: Westview.

Fukuyama, F. (2001) 'Social capital, civil society and development', *Third World Quarterly*, 22 (1).

Galanter, M., Castameda, R. and Salamon, I. (1987) 'Institutional self help therapy for alcoholism: clinical outcome', *Alcohol Clinical and Experimental Research*, 11: 424–9.

Gavrielides, T. (2007) *Restorative justice theory and practice: Addressing the discrepancy*, Helsinki: HEUNI.

Gavrielides, T. (2014) 'Reconciling the notions of restorative justice and imprisonment', *The Prison Journal*, 94(4): 479–505, http://tpj.sagepub.com/content/early/2014/09/01. 0032885514548010

Gill, A.J., French, R.M., Gergle, D. and Oberlander, J. (2008)'The language of emotion in short blog texts', proceedings of the 2008 ACM Conference on Computer Supported Cooperative Work, ACM, pp 299–302.

Giordano, P.C., Cernkovich, S.A. and Rudolph, J.L. (2002) 'Gender, crime and desistance: Towards a theory of cognitive transformation', *American Journal of Sociology*, 107: 990–1064.

Good, M., Good, B., Schaffer, C. and Lind, S (1990) 'American oncology and the discourse of hope', *Cultural Medicine and Psychiatry*, 14: 59–79.

Granfield, R., & Cloud, W. (1999) *Coming clean: Overcoming addiction without treatment*, New York: New York University Press.

Granfield, R. and Cloud, W. (2001) 'Social context and "natural recovery": the role of social capital in the resolution of drug-associated problems', *Substance Use and Misuse*, 36: 1543–70.

Groshkova, T., Best, D. and White, W. (2011) 'Recovery Group Participation Scale (RGPS): factor structure in alcohol and heroin recovery populations', *Journal of Groups in Addiction and Recovery*, 6: 76–92.

Groshkova, T., Best, D. and White, W. (2012) 'The assessment of recovery capital: properties and psychometrics of a measure of addiction recovery strengths', *Drug and Alcohol Review*, 32(2):187–94.

Haslam, C., Jetten, J., Cruwys, T., Dingle, G. and Haslam, A. (2018) *The New Psychology of Health: Unlocking the Social Cure*, Abingdon, Oxon: Routledge.

Haslam, S.A. (2014) 'Making good theory practical: Five lessons for an Applied Social Identity Approach to challenges of organizational, health, and clinical psychology', *British Journal of Social Psychology*, 53(1): 1–20.

Haslam, S.A. and Reicher, S. (2006) 'Stressing the group: social identity and the unfolding dynamics of responses to stress', *The Journal of Applied Psychology*, 91(5): 1037–52.

Haslam, S.A., Reicher, S.D. and Levine, M. (2012) 'When other people are heaven, when other people are hell: How social identity determines the nature and impact of social support', in J. Jetten, C. Haslam and S.A. Haslam (eds), *The Social Cure: Identity, Health and Well-being*, New York: Psychology Press, pp 157–74.

Haslam, A., Jetten, J., Postmes, T. and Haslam, C. (2017) 'Social identity, health and wellbeing: An emerging agenda for applied psychology', *Applied Psychology*, 58(1): 1–23.

Hirschfield, P.J. and Piquero, A.R. (2010) 'Normalization and legitimation: Modeling stigmatizing attitudes toward ex-offenders', *Criminology*, 48(1): 27–55.

Hobbs, W.R., Burke, M., Christakis, N.A. and Fowler, J.H. (2016) 'Online social integration is associated with reduced mortality risk', *Proceedings of the National Academy of Sciences of the United States of America*, 113(46): 12980–4.

Hughes, R. (1999) '"Clean" or "dirty": drug injectors' perceptions of cleanliness and dirtiness in relation to HIV risk behaviour', *Addiction Research*, 7(5): 433–445.

Humphreys, K. and Lembke, A. (2013) 'Recovery-oriented policy and care systems in the United Kingdom and United States', *Drug and Alcohol Review*, 33(1): 13–18.

Hunter, B.A., Lanza, A.S., Lawlor, M., Dyson, W. and Gordon, D.M. (2016) 'A strengths-based approach to prisoner reentry: the Fresh Start Prisoner Reentry Program', *International Journal of Offender Therapy and Comparative Criminology*, 60(11): 1298–314, doi: 10.1177/0306624X15576501

Jasinskaja-Lahti, I., Liebkind, K., Jaakola, M. and Jaakola Reuter, A. (2006) 'Perceived discrimination, social support networks and psychological wellbeing among three immigrant groups', *Journal of Cross-Cultural Psychology*, 37: 293–311.

Jason, L., Olson, B., Ferrari, J., Majer, J., Alvarez, J. and Stout, J. (2007) 'An examination of main and interactive effects of substance abuse recovery housing on multiple indicators of adjustment', *Addiction*, 102: 1114–21.

Jetten, J., Haslam, C. and Haslam S.A. (eds) (2012a) *The Social Cure: Identity, Health and Well-being*, New York: Psychology Press.

Jetten, J., Haslam, S.A. and Haslam, C. (2012b) 'The case for a social identity analysis of health and well-being', in J. Jetten, C. Haslam and S.A. Haslam (eds), *The Social Cure: Identity, Health and Well-being*, New York: Psychology Press, pp 3–19.

Jetten, J., Branscombe, N., Haslam, S., Haslam, C., Cruwys, T., Jones, J. and Zhang, A. (2015) 'Having a lot of a good thing: Multiple important group memberships as a source of self-esteem', *PLoS One*, 10(6): e0131035.

Jones, R., Simonson, P. and Singleton, N. (2010) *Experiences of Stigma – Everyday Barriers for Drug Users and their Families*, London: UK Drug Policy Commission, www.ukdpc.org.uk

Kaskutas, L.A., Bond, J. and Avalos, L.A. (2009) '7-year trajectories of Alcoholics Anonymous attendance and associations with treatment', *Addictive Behaviors*, 34(12): 1029–35.

Kelly, J. and White, W. (2011) *Addiction Recovery Management: Theory, Research and Practice*, Humana Press: New York.

Kelly, J.F. and Yeterian, J.D. (2008) 'Mutual-help groups', in W. O'Donohue and J.R. Cunningham (eds), *Evidence-based Adjunctive Treatments*, New York: Elsevier, pp 61–105.

Kretzmann, J. and McKnight, J. (1993) *Building Communities from the Inside Out: A Path Toward Finding and Mobilising a Community's Assets*, Skokie, IL: ACTA Publications.

Lacey, N. and Pickard, H. (2015) 'To blame or to forgive? Reconciling punishment and forgiveness in criminal justice', *Oxford Journal of Legal Studies*, 35(4): 665–96.

Laub, J. and Sampson, R. (2003) *Shared Beginnings: Divergent Lives: Delinquent Boys to Age 70*, Cambridge, MA: Harvard University Press.

Laub, J.H., Nagin, D.S. and Sampson, R.J. (1998) 'Trajectories of change in criminal offending: good marriages and the desistance process', *American Sociological Review*, 63: 225–38.

Laub, J. H., Sampson, R.J. and Sweeten, G.A. (2006)'Assessing Sampson and Laub's Life-Course Theory of Crime', in F.T. Cullen, J.P. Wright and K.R. Blevins (eds), *Advances in criminological theory: Vol. 15. Taking stock: The status of criminological theory*, Piscataway, NJ, US: Transaction Publishers, pp 313–333.

Laws, R. and Ward, T. (2011) *Desistance from Sex Offending: Alternatives to Throwing Away the Key*, New York: Guildford Press.

Leamy, M., Bird, V., Le Boutillier, C., Williams, J. and Slade, M. (2011) 'A conceptual framework for personal recovery in mental health: systematic review and narrative synthesis', *British Journal of Psychiatry*, 199: 445–52.

Link, B.G. and Phelan, J.C. (2001) 'Conceptualizing stigma', *Annual Review of Sociology*, 27(1): 363–85.

Litt, M.D., Kadden, R.M., Kabela-Cormier, E. and Petry, N. (2007) 'Changing network support for drinking: Initial findings from the Network Support Project', *Journal of Consulting and Clinical Psychology*, 75(4): 542.

Litt, M., Kadden, R.M., Kabela-Cormier, E. and Petry, N. (2009) 'Changing network support for drinking: Network Support Project two-year follow-up', *Journal of Consulting and Clinical Psychology*, 77 (2): 229–242.

Llewellyn, J., Archibald, B., Clairmont, D. and Crocker, D. (2013) 'Imagining Success for a Restorative Approach to Justice: Implications for Measurement and Evaluation', *Dalhousie Law Journal*, 36(2): 281–316.

Longabaugh, R., Wirtz, P.W., Zywiak, W.H. and O'Malley, S.S. (2010) 'Network support as a prognostic indicator of drinking outcomes: The COMBINE study', *Journal of Studies on Alcohol and Drugs*, 71(6): 837.

MacLin, M.K. and Herrera, V. (2006) 'The criminal stereotype', *North American Journal of Psychology*, 8(2): 197–208.

Manning, V., Best, D., Faulkner, N., Titherington, E., Morinan, A., Keaney, F., Gossop, M. and Strang, J. (2012) 'Does active referral by a doctor or 12-step peer improve 12-step meeting attendance? Results from a pilot Randomised Control Trial', *Drug and Alcohol Dependence*, 126(1): 131–7.

Markson, L., Losel, F., Souza, K. and Lanskey, C. (2015) 'Male prisoners' family relationships and resilience in resettlement', *Criminology & Criminal Justice*, 15(4): 423–41.

Marmot, M., Allen, J., Goldblatt, P., Boyce, T., McNeish, D., Grady, M. and Geddes, I. (2010) *Fair Society, Healthy Lives: A Strategic Review of Inequalities in England Post-2010*, London: University College London.

Maruna, S. (2001) *Making Good: How Ex-Convicts Reform and Rebuild Their Lives*, Washington, DC: American Psychological Association.

Maruna, S. (2012) 'Elements of successful desistance signalling', *Criminology and Public Policy*, 11(1): 73–86.

Maruna, S. and Farrall, S. (2004) 'Desistance from crime: A theoretical reformulation', *Kolner Zeitschrift fur Sozologie und Sozialpsychologie*, 43: 171–94.

McIntosh, J. and McKeganey, N. (2000) 'Addicts' narratives of recovery from drug use: constructing a non-addict identity', *Social Science & Medicine*, 50: 1501–10.

McIntosh, J. and McKeganey, N. (2002) *Beating the Dragon: The Recovery from Dependent Drug Use*, London: Prentice Hall.

McKnight, J. (1995) *The Careless Society: Community and its Counterfeits*, New York: Basic Books.

McKnight, J. and Block, P. (2010) *The Abundant Community: Awakening the Power of Families and Neighbourhoods*, San Francisco: Berrett-Koehler Publishers Inc.

McNeill, F. (2014) 'Discovering desistance: Three aspects of desistance?' http://blogs.irss.org.uk/discovering desistance/2014/05/23/three-aspects-of-desistance/

McNeill, F., Batchelor, F., Burnett, R. and Knox, J. (2005) '21st century social work', in *Reducing Re-Offending: Key Practice Skills*, Edinburgh: Scottish Executive.

Mericle, A., Miles, J. and Cacciola, J. (2015) 'A critical component of the continuum of care for substance use disorders: Recovery homes in Philadelphia', *Journal of Psychoactive Drugs*, 47(1): 80–90.

Moos, R.H. (2007) 'Theory-based active ingredients of effective treatments for substance use disorders', *Drug and Alcohol Dependence*, 88(2–3): 109–21.

Naser, R.L. and La Vigne, N.G. (2006) 'Family support in the prisoner reentry process: expectations and realities', *Journal of Offender Rehabilitation*, 43: 93–106.

National Audit Office (2010) 'Managing offenders on short custodial sentences', London: The Stationery Office.

Neale, J., Nettleton, S. and Pickering, L. (2011) 'What is the role of harm reduction when drug users say they want abstinence?' *International Journal of Drug Policy*, 22(3): 189–193.

Nutbrown, C., Bishop, J. and Wheeler, H. (2015) 'Co-production of family literacy projects to enhance early literacy development', *Journal of Children's Services*, 10(3): 265–79, https://doi.org/10.1108/JCS-02-2015-0011

OECD (2007) *Human Capital: How What you Know Shapes your Life*, Paris: Organisation for Economic Co-operation and Development.

Paternoster, R. and Bushway, S. (2009) 'Desistance and the 'feared self': Towards an identity theory of criminal desistance', *Journal of Criminal Law and Criminology*, 99(4): 1103–56.

Pennebaker, J.W. (2011) *The Secret Life of Pronouns: What Our Words Say About Us*, New York: Bloomsbury Press.

Pestoff, V., Brandsen, T. and Verschuere, B. (eds) (2010) *New Public Governance, the Third Sector and Co-production*, London: Routledge.

Phillips, L.A. and Shaw, A. (2013) 'Substance use more stigmatized than smoking and obesity', *Journal of Substance Use*, 18(4): 247–53.

Putnam, R. (1995) 'Bowling alone: America's declining social capital', *Journal of Democracy*, 6(1): 65–78.

Putnam, R.D. (2000) *Bowling Alone: The Collapse and Revival of American Community*, London: Simon & Schuster.

Putnam, R.D. and Feldstein, L. (2004) *Better Together: Restoring the American Community*, New York: Simon and Schuster.

Radcliffe, P. (2011) 'Motherhood, pregnancy, and the negotiation of identity: The moral career of drug treatment', *Social Science & Medicine*, 72(6): 984–91.

RETHINK (2008) *Getting back into the world: Reflections on lived experiences of recovery*, London, UK: RETHINK.

Rex, S. (1999) 'Desistance from offending: experiences of probation', *The Howard Journal of Criminal Justice*, 38(4): 366–83.

Riessman, F. (1965) 'The helper therapy principle', *Social Work*, 10(2): 27–32.

Rocque, M., Bierie, D.M., Posick, C. and MacKenzie, D.L. (2013) 'Unraveling change: social bonds and recidivism among released offenders', *Victims and Offenders*, 8: 209–30.

Rodham, K., McCabe, C. and Blake, D. (2009) 'Seeking support: An interpretative phenomenological analysis of an Internet message board for people with Complex Regional Pain Syndrome', *Psychology and Health*, 24(6): 619–34.

Ronel, N., and Segev, D. (eds) (2015) *Positive Criminology*, Abingdon, Oxon: Routledge.

Rosenquist, J.N., Murabito, J., Fowler, J.H. and Christakis, N.A. (2010) 'The spread of alcohol consumption behavior in a large social network', *Annals of internal medicine*, 152(7): 426–W141.

Roth, J. and Best, D. (eds) (2013) *Addiction and Recovery in the UK*, Abingdon, Oxon: Routledge.

Saleeby, D. (1996) 'The strengths perspective in social work practice: Extensions and cautions', *Social Work*, 41: 296–305.

Sampson, R.J. and Laub, J.H. (1992) 'Crime and deviance in the life course', *Annual Review of Sociology*, 18: 63–84.

Sampson, R.J. and Laub, J.H. (2003) 'Life-course desisters? Trajectories of crime among delinquent boys followed to age 70*', *Criminology*, 41(3): 555–92.

Savic, M., Best, D., Rodda, S. and Lubman, D.I. (2013) 'Exploring the focus and experiences of smartphone applications for addiction recovery', *Journal of Addictive Diseases*, 32(3): 310–19.

Scott, J. (2012) *Social Network Analysis*, London: Sage.

Sheedy, C. and Whitter, M. (2009) 'Guiding principles and elements of recovery-oriented systems of care: what do we know from the research?' HHS Publication No (SMA) 09-4439, Rockville, MD: Center for Substance Abuse Treatment, Substance Abuse and Mental Health Services Administration.

Shneiderman, B. (2008) 'Copernican challenges face those who suggest that collaboration, not computation are the driving energy for socio-technical systems that characterize Web 2.0', *Science*, 319: 1349–50.

Sloan, J. (2012) '"You can see your face in my floor": examining the function of cleanliness in an adult male prison', *Howard Journal of Criminal Justice*, 51(4): 400–10.

Snyder, C. (2000) *Handbook of Hope: Theory, Measures and Applications*, San Diego, CA: Academic Press.

Tajfel, H. and Turner, J.C. (1979) 'An integrative theory of intergroup conflict', in W.G. Austin and S. Worchel (eds), *The Social Psychology of Intergroup Relations*, Monterey, CA: Brooks/Cole, pp 33–47.

Timko, C., DeBenedetti, A. and Billow, R. (2006) 'Intensive referral to 12-step self-help groups and 6-month substance use disorder outcomes', *Addiction*, 101(5): 678–88.

Turner, J. (1991) *Social Influence*, Buckingham, UK: Open University Press, and Belmont, CA: Wadsworth Publishing.

UK Drug Policy Commission (2008) *The UK Drug Policy Commission Recovery Consensus Group: A Vision of Recovery*, London: UK Drug Policy Commission.

UK Drug Policy Commission (2010) *Getting Serious About Stigma: The Problem With Stigmatising Drug Users: An Overview*, https://goo.gl/XH4MSy

Ward, T. and Stewart, C.A. (2003) 'The treatment of sex offenders: risk management and good lives', *Professional Psychology: Research and Practice*, 34(4): 353–60.

Weaver, B. (2016) *Offending and Desistance: The Importance of Social Relations*, Abingdon, Oxon: Routledge.

Wexler, D. (1999) 'Therapeutic jurisprudence: an overview', presentation at Thomas Cooley Disabilities Law Review Lay Symposium, East Lansing, MI, 29 October.

White, W. (2006) *Pathways from the Culture of Addiction to the Culture of Recovery: A Travel Guide for Addiction Professionals*, Hazelden: Betty Ford.

White, W. (2009) *Peer-based Addiction Recovery Support: History, Theory, Practice, and Scientific Evaluation*, Chicago, IL: Great Lakes Addiction Technology Transfer Center and Philadelphia Department of Behavioral Health and Mental Retardation Services.

White, W. (2012) *Recovery/Remission from Substance Use Disorders: An Analysis of Reported Outcomes in 415 Scientific Reports*, Philadelphia, PA: Philadelphia Department of Behavioural Health and Intellectual Disability Services and the Great Lakes Addiction Technology Transfer Center.

White, W. (2017) *Recovery Rising*, Punta Gorda, FL: Rita Chaney.

Wilton, R. and DeVerteuil, G. (2006) 'Spaces of sobriety/sites of power: Examining social model alcohol recovery programs as therapeutic landscapes', *Social Science and Medicine*, 63: 649–61.

Williams, A. (1999) 'Introduction', in A. Williams (ed), *Therapeutic Landscapes: The Dynamics Between Place and Wellness*, Lanham, MA: University Press of America, pp 1–11.

Wolff, N. and Draine, J. (2004) 'Dynamics of social capital of prisoners and community reentry: ties that bind', *Journal of Correctional Health Care*, 10(3): 457–90.

World Health Organization (2001) *The World Health Report. Mental Health: New Understandings, New Hope*, Geneva.

Zehr, H. and Gohar, A. (2002) *Little Book of Restorative Justice*, Pennsylvania: Good Books.

Zhang, Z., Friedmann, P.D. and Gerstein, D.R. (2003) 'Does retention matter? Treatment duration and improvement in drug use', *Addiction*, 98(5): 673–84.

Zoorob, M. and Salemi, J. (2017) 'Bowling alone, dying together: The role of social capital in mitigating the drug overdose epidemic in the United States', *Drug and Alcohol Dependence*, 173: 1–9.

Zywiak, W., Neighbors, C., Martin, R., Johnson, J., Eaton, C. and Rosenhow, D. (2009) 'The important people drug and alcohol interview: Psychometric properties, predictive validity and implications for treatment', *Journal of Substance Abuse Treatment*, 36(3): 321–30.

Index

J

K

L

M

N

O

P

U

V

W

Y

Z

Printed and bound by CPI Group (UK) Ltd, Croydon, CR0 4YY

09/06/2025

14685897-0001